Early North American
DOLLMAKING

A Narrative History and Craft Instructions

Early North American
DOLLMAKING

A Narrative History and Craft Instructions

IRIS SANDERSON JONES

DRAWINGS: CATHERINE CLAYTOR-BECKER
PHOTOGRAPHS: MICKY JONES

101 PRODUCTIONS
SAN FRANCISCO

"To Micky, of course."

Printed and bound in the United States of America

Distributed to the book trade in the United States
by Charles Scribner's Sons, New York, and in Canada
by Van Nostrand Reinhold Ltd., Toronto

Published by 101 Productions
834 Mission Street
San Francisco, California 94103

Library of Congress Cataloging in Publication Data

Jones, Iris Sanderson, 1932-
    Early North American dollmaking.

    Includes index.
    1. Dollmaking.   2. Dolls--North America--His-
tory. I. Title.   745.59'22   76-44413
TT175.J66
ISBN O-89286-107-X
ISBN O-89286-108-8 pbk.

CONTENTS

ACKNOWLEDGEMENTS

The story of dolls in the United States and Canada was like a giant jigsaw puzzle slowly pieced together with the help of several hundred museums and doll collectors. I am grateful to Henry Ford Museum in Dearborn, Michigan, especially to Douglas Hough and Timothy Prouty, Crafts; Henry Prebys, Design and Display; George Byrd, Decorative Arts; David Glick, Education; Mary Woolever, Textiles; and Donald Adams, Public Relations. Special thanks also to Margaret Whitton of the Margaret Woodbury Strong Museum; dollmakers Barbara Coker, Meredith Hollingsworth, Theresa Little and Helen Bullard; Dennis Greenall and Philip Tilney of the National Museums of Canada; Henry Figgins of the National Gallery of Art; Lorraine O'Byrne of Black Creek Pioneer Village; Sandra Neidy of the Canadian Government Office of Tourism; Artist William Breitmeyer; Researcher Gail Cole; and my Assistant Barbara Young, who helped to write the demonstrations and the Georgian scene on page 61.

Credits: Margaret Woodbury Strong Museum, Rochester, New York, dolls pp. 14, 15, 27, 33, 36, 37, 95-107, 118; Barbara Coker, dolls pp. 41 (B), 90, 126, 127, 129, 131, 135 and cover as well as demonstrations pp. 39-68, 124, 132, 133; Rare Book Division of The New York Public Library, Astor, Lenox and Tilden Foundations engraving p. 24; National Museums of Canada photos pp. 32, 75 (L.), and Nos. 11-15 on pp. 77, 78; Winifred Covintree, doll p. 41 (A) and cover; Black Creek Pioneer Village, Metropolitan Toronto and Region Conservation Authority, Percy Band Collection photos Nos. 1-10, pp. 72-76; Mrs. C. E. Steele, doll No. 16, p. 78; Esther Martin Sittler, doll No. 17, p. 78, photo University of Toronto Fine Arts Archives; Nancy Lou Patterson, dolls Nos. 18, 19, p. 79, photo University of Waterloo Fine Arts Archives; National Gallery of Art, Washington, Index of American Design, photos Nos. 1-27, pp. 82-93; Meredith Hollingsworth, dolls demonstrated pp. 110-117 and cover; Theresa Little, dolls pp. 119-125; Lynn Rogers, doll p. 134.

PART ONE

DOLLS OF PLANET EARTH

IMAGES

There is a star two-thirds of the way across the Milky Way galaxy. It is a small sun, one of many in the universe encircled by planets: small planets, gas giants, middle planets. On one of the smaller planets, hot lava and gases cooled long ago to form sculptured red rock landscapes, areas of huge thick-stemmed plants that rise upward for one hundred feet and mountainous ridges covered with snow.

Plants and animals, in strange and exotic shapes and colors, live on this planet, among them creatures who think and design and pray. In our language we would call them "people." They come in many colors: delicate shades of yellow and beige and brown; warm reds; deep blacks. They share with other living creatures of the small planet a need to eat the food of the environment to survive, and to reproduce themselves in kind, but they also possess qualities that no other creatures on the planet possess. They make great shouting noises of joy and strange gurgling sounds of sadness. They are afraid, not only when the enemy is upon them, but when there is no enemy in sight; they picture the enemy in their heads and tremble. They see their own shapes, and the shapes of other living things, in trees and rocks, and even in the ripe fruit hanging from the trees. They imagine creatures from other places, unseen but powerful, living in clouds and on high, inaccessible mountaintops.

These creatures of the small planet have another trait that other animals share only to a limited degree: curiosity. Why does the great plant grow up towards the sun instead of sideways along the ground? Why does the blue liquid sea roll the rocks back and forth forever across the edge of the land? Why does the hunt go well one day, so that the great creature with the horned tusks is killed, and badly another day so there is no food? Why do the "people" hurt and die when there is no food?

The small planet, in its galaxy of stars, is a world that the people who live on it cannot control. It is not enough to be strong, or even clever. The gods who live on the mountaintop and other high places control the world; the people are merely puppets. The people need a puppet world of their own, a world where they can learn to cope with a hostile environment and eventually control it. They need magic.

On this strange and wondrous place of red rock plateaus and giant trees, the people of many colors find magic in many places. They find it on the edge of the sea, where the water rubs driftwood trees against the shore rocks at the foot of the forest. They find figures in the driftwood and in the trees themselves. In other places, by a fire perhaps, the figure is seen in a stone at the edge of the burning fire. If the stone is hot, is the man in the stone burning? If the forces that rule the world put magic figures in the image of a

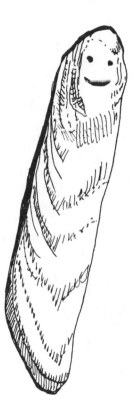

man, in wood and stone, is this not a message? Are the figures clearer if the people rub them with a sharp stone? Can one make a figure come out of the stone, or out of wood, with his own hands? Did the hunt go well the day after he found the shape of a man in wood? Did the crops grow in rain when the stone image was placed in the field?

So it is that the many-colored people who live on a small planet called Earth, near a star two-thirds of the way across the Milky Way galaxy, learn to make images of themselves and to use those images to control the world. It happens independently in all parts of the planet, on the icy slopes, on the sculptured plains, in the jungles, and even on the islands of the sea. As the planet changes and ages, and many people learn new ways of controlling their environment, wise men of the Earth talk of images made to control the gods and images made for the play of children, but there is no difference. The people who live in remote places or in small tribes make images because they need magic. The people who live in cities make images for museums and churches and call them art. Children, from every part of the planet, use images to create a fantasy place where they can learn about the world and control it; it is called play.

In other parts of the universe, where our telescope eyes see only the gleam of light, the "people" may be made of long white feathers or purple blocks of living stone. In those places, I am sure, they make dolls in their own image, as do the people of Earth.

DOLLS OF PLANET EARTH

"What is the name of this planet?"
"It is called Earth."
"My planet circles the double sun on the other side of the galaxy. I have not seen Earth before. Are you an Earth creature?"
"We are called people."
"What do you hold in your hand, people?"
"That is a doll."
"What is a doll?"
"A doll is . . .

All over the Earth, in different times and places, human beings have recreated the world in their own image. We use sharp stones to carve driftwood or chunks of trees. We chip faces from stone, and weave figures from grass. We make dolls from bone and from the fruit of trees.

We make dolls to encourage the birth of a child and to bury beside him in the tomb. We craft them to win rain from the sky, to celebrate the harvest, to seek vengeance and as a substitute for human sacrifice. We do not know how long the people have made dolls, but we have found centuries-old rag dolls stuffed with papyrus leaves from the Nile and dolls in the tombs of ancient Egyptians. They have been made beyond memory in Asia.

"Do all people make them? Is it instinct?"
"No. We have found no Stone Age dolls."
"Stone Age?"
"They are the people who used sharp stones for weapons and tools. They did not discover metal. We know about Stone Age men in Africa and the South Pacific and in the caves of Europe. The cave men painted the figures of their animal enemies on the wall, and killed them with a painted spear."

"They did not chip dolls with their sharpened stones?"

"Nobody knows. Dollmaking goes back so far that nobody really knows."

The first European explorers in Africa found small wooden dolls in many places. Children used them. Virgins and childless women carried them. In ancient Japan, the Japanese left simple sticks, with wood shavings for hair, on the banks of rivers during purification ceremonies. Mothers carried them to protect their children from evil. We call these dolls "scapegoats," a Jewish word for the custom of investing a goat with the qualities of a man so that the goat instead of the man will be blamed for transgressions against the gods. It was very common to sacrifice human beings as a token of esteem to the gods, until the day came when dolls were substituted for men. The Mongols used dolls to save people from disease: the doll was "given" the disease and then invited to ride away on a birchbark horse.

In Africa, Haiti, South America, and sometimes among black people in the United States, dolls were used for voodoo: Men and women destroyed the person by destroying the doll. Witchcraft was also practiced in seventeenth-century Scotland, as this description by a witch of that time called Isobel Gowdie describes:

> "John Taylor brought home the clay in his plaid; his wife broke it very small, like meal, and sifted it in a sieve and poured water among it in the devil's name and wrought it very sore, like a rye-bowt and made of it a picture of the Laird's son. It had all the parts and marks of a child, such as head, eyes, nose, hands, feet, mouth and little lips. It wanted no mark of a child; and the hands of it folded by its sides. [The witch roasted the doll to bring on a fatal fever in the child.]"

"So the people of planet Earth make dolls for magic reasons?"

"Well yes, but most of us use them nowadays for play!"

"Play?"

"How on earth can I describe play?"

All the children of the earth love to race and jump and make a noise for no apparent reason. Do they have too much energy, too much exuberance, or is it instinct? No one really knows. We do know that through play we explore and experiment and make social arrangements with one another. Experiments have shown certain recurring traits among animals, and some of the conclusions drawn can be applied to people. Play includes the emotional element of pleasure. It often has no immediate practical value. There is more playfulness in the immature than in the mature animal, and it is more common among higher animals than it is among lower animals. Play seems to be a highly developed skill.

We learn through play. We learn mental and manipulative skills by playing with any natural or man-made material in the environment. Pleasure sticks like golf clubs and hockey sticks and billiard cues were once the weapons of long ago. Chinese firecrackers are the gunpowder of war. One of the world's ancient toys is the ball, probably created from an ideal natural shape. Another ancient toy is the doll. It was not a toy until long after it was used for religious purposes, although children have probably always made "people figures" from sticks and stones.

Congo girls carry a piece of wood as a "child" on their backs. In Angola they use corncobs with wax breasts and rag clothes, and in other parts of Africa they tie a gourd in the middle as it grows to make the shape of a man. Indians give silver-decked dolls to adolescent brides. Scandinavians whittle wooden toys. The British make corn dolls to celebrate the harvest. Asians dedicate worn-out dolls to the deities. Even among Islamic people, whose religion forbids the reproduction of the human image as an idol, there is the story of nine-year-old Ayesta, bride of Mohammed, who brought her dolls into the harem, where she and Mohammed played with the dolls together.

Dolls were used for magic and dolls were used for play. . .

"It is the same, is it not?"

"The same?"

"When a man uses a doll to protect him from the gods, or a woman uses a doll to bring her a child, they are trying to understand a world they cannot control. When the child uses a doll for play, doesn't he also use it in a world he cannot control? Are there no stories of people who use dolls to learn how to be hunters, or of people who use them for both magic and play?"

"There is the story of the Hopi Kachina . . ."

INDIAN AND ESKIMO DOLLS

If we could focus a camera on the Indians and Eskimos of North America during the periods before and after "the coming of the white man," we would see the transition from ritual to play in action. The Hopi Indians, one of the Pueblo tribes of the southwestern United States, have long known that play is the work of the child. Their Kachina dolls were traditionally used to educate children through play. The Hopis appear to be the only one of the Indian or Eskimo tribes to have made dolls for play before the Europeans came to North America. Native Americans were highly skilled in the artistic use of stone, wood, bone, shell and clay, however, so it did not take them long to adapt their skills to dollmaking once the Europeans arrived.

THE HOPIS

Focus the camera on a Hopi village during the time of the Spanish *conquistadores*. Apartments are built one above the other in the dusty red rocks of the Southwest desert. In a high room, where the family is gathered to eat, a Kachina doll looks down from a shelf. Father, who is a farmer, comes out of the high room, down a ladder to the ground. In the corn field he digs carefully with a pointed tool to plant the corn, which must be protected against the crows and the worms and the weather while it waits for rain. The gods who live on

the mountaintops to the west have created the sculptured red rock landscape, as well as the snake and the eagle which inhabit the land; the gods who live on the mountains will also bring rain.

In the village, the sculptor of Kachina dolls wears a band of cloth around his head. It makes a colorful streak against the red stone face of the high houses and the rock ledge on which he sits. He begins with a suitable piece of wood, the round trunk of a cottonwood tree cut about one foot long. As he works, he chisels the shape of the body and the features of the doll, and then adds a separate wooden headdress, intricately carved. He sands the doll with a piece of sandstone from the earth and paints the doll with the natural dyes of the earth: roots, juices, ashes and plant fibers.

It is not easy for outsiders to understand the complicated ritual significance of "Kachinas." Adult Kachina dancers, wearing masks that represent a variety of supernatural spirits, stomp out their sacred dances in woven costumes and soft leather boots. The dancers represent the spirit of the gods. Kachina dolls, which are miniature wooden versions of the masked Kachina dancers, have no such spiritual significance; they are carved to teach the child the names and the spiritual value of the gods represented in the dance. There may be more than three hundred different Kachina figures for the child to learn: Kachinas that represent the spirit of the wind and the thunder and the earth and the animals.

Is this ritual or is it play? If play is the work of the child, a wise man might see very little difference.

THE ESKIMOS

Shift the scene now, several thousand miles to the north, a century after the white traders made contact with the Eskimos. You see a small figure who wears one suit of fur next to his skin and a second suit with fur turned out against the arctic wind. To the rest of the world this small figure is only a doll, but to the girl child who made him he is a true hunter. The child made the doll's clothes under her mother's supervision, scraping the hide and sewing the clothes with bone needles and sinew. This is a dramatic form of play, but to the Eskimo child it represents what playthings are to every child—working tools.

Survival on these frozen slopes creates specific roles for each member of the family. An Eskimo man in this environment cannot live without a wife, because she prepares the skins and the food and trains the children for a hunter's life. Girls must be taught to chew the sealskins until they are soft enough for boots, to scrape and sew the caribou furs for clothes and to cook over an open fire. Father is the hunter and provider. He needs sons to join him in the hunt.

A young boy also learns through play. He builds his own little igloo, carefully cutting blocks of snow and shaping them into a house. He sleds down the snowed slopes, crashing in a laughing heap against the nearest icy ridge. He pretends that he is a husky dog, harnessed and pulling his brothers and sisters on a sled, and he dreams of the day when he will be a hunter like his father, with his own team of dogs. In the spring, when water begins to run in dark roads through the ice, he plays at being a hunter, chasing small animals and birds that are always faster than he is. At night he listens to the storyteller recount tales of the great hunt. He knows that the

walrus gets bigger and the danger greater each time the story is told but he doesn't care; for the moment he is the hunter, harpooning the animal as bravely as any hunter before him. When winter comes again, his father will teach him how to set traps in the snow, digging a hole for the trap and covering it carefully with blocks of snow. Eventually he will go with the men when the dogs pull a small boat on a sled to the water's edge for the seal hunt. On that day, when he kills his first seal he will be a man. A man dressed exactly like the "doll hunter" made by his sister during long days beside the fire.

This picture of the Eskimo family was true in the centuries after the first explorers came to North America, and it is still true in many places today. Eskimo life was a life of isolation, so much so that these northern hunters had no other name for themselves than "Inuit," which means literally, the People.

NINETEENTH CENTURY ALASKA

As the years went by, the People made dolls of fur, sealskin, gut, feathers, fish skin, wood and stone. By 1896, Edward William Nelson reported to the Canadian government that "Along the Alaskan shore wherever I went, as well as along the Yukon and Kuskokwim Rivers and on Nunivak Island, dolls were found in common use. They are usually small images of wood, ivory or bone. . . . While making a brief visit to Sledge Island, two little girls in the house where we stopped amused us by watching their opportunity, while we were busy among other things, to place their dolls standing in a semicircle before us upon the floor, while they sat quietly behind as though permitting their dolls to take a look at the strangers. In connection with these toys, girls have also a complete outfit of toy bedding made from the skins of mice or lemmings, small grass mats, toy boots, mittens and clothing, all patterned after those used by the People of the locality."

DOLLS DISCOVER AMERICA

Sir Walter Raleigh carried a shipment of Elizabethan dolls to the New World when he colonized Virginia in 1585. De Bry's *America,* published in Frankfurt in 1590, contains an excellent illustration (see chapter illustration) of an Indian child carrying one of those dolls. Beneath the engraving, which is based on a painting by John White, an eyewitness journalist comments that the Indians were "greatlye Diligted with puppetts, and babes which wear brought oute of England."

I watched a modern version of that scene in 1976, nearly 400 years after the Virginian expedition, when a surgeon in Mount Sinai Hospital in Michigan made a doll from a surgical glove for a restless child. The surgeon inflated the glove and tied it like a balloon, forming a head topped with four fingers and a thumb. He deftly drew a face on the doll, with a felt pen, and topped it with a disposable paper cap, greatly delighting the child with a "puppett," or maybe it was a "babe," of his own.

These two scenes reflect the two doll traditions that have persisted in North America since the first colonists: the traditions of the imported commercial doll and the spur-of-the-moment home-made doll. All commercial dolls were imported from Europe until the first small dollmaking industries began on this continent in the mid-nineteenth century. Simple dolls of available materials were made by individuals at home for the three centuries preceding that time. Homemade dolls continued to dominate the playrooms of the United States and Canada until early in the twentieth century.

The exploration of the New World and the development of play dolls were concurrent events, because both grew out of the age of exploration that followed the Middle Ages. The Renaissance means literally the "rebirth"; it was the end of an era when people looked only inward at their souls, and the beginning of an era when people looked outward, at the world around them. There was a new openness and creativity. This was the world that stimulated Michelangelo, Da Vinci and Gutenberg. It was also the world that sent explorers around Cape Horn, the Cape of Good Hope and across the Atlantic to find a new route to the Orient. We have found a few dolls buried in Roman tombs, but there is no record of everyday professional dollmaking until the fourteenth century, when European fishermen were beginning to fish the waters off Newfoundland.

Woodcuts show craftsmen making dolls in Europe in 1491, one year before Christopher Columbus of Genoa landed on San Salvador under the Spanish flag and six years before John Cabot of Venice landed on Newfoundland under the British flag. Dolls became the royal rage of Europe during the next hundred years, when French and Spanish explorers were probing the coastlines and waterways of North America. Emperor Charles the Fifth ordered a doll for his daughter from Paris in 1530, for the outrageous sum of ten francs, in spite of his ongoing political war with France. The Duchess of Lorraine presented six exquisitely dressed "babes" to her newborn granddaughter, the Duchess of Bavaria in 1570. The clothing of these dolls

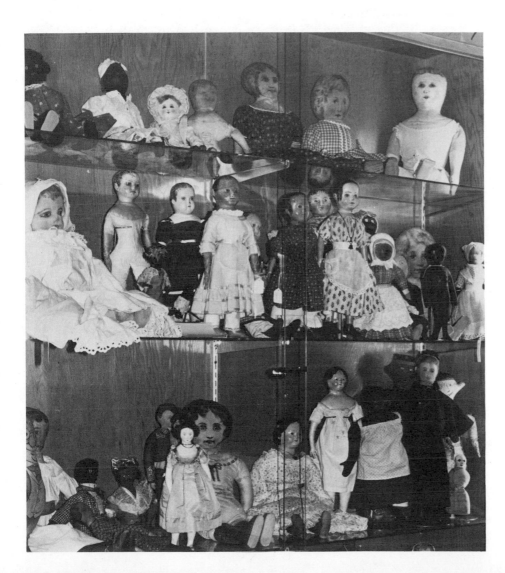

was suitably regal, but the bodies were often nothing more than a bundle of rags or a leather pouch filled with sawdust. This was the century when three important names were written on the vague outlines of a North American map. The Spanish founded St. Augustine. The British founded Jamestown. And Jacques Cartier sailed up the St. Lawrence River, noting "Quebec—the place where the river narrows."

By the seventeenth century, when British, French and Spanish colonists settled Massachussetts, New France and Santa Fe, wealthy European families were collecting exquisite miniatures and placing them in finely crafted cabinets that were out of the reach of children. One hundred years later, when the British beat the French on the Plains of Abraham and lost their eastern seabord colonies to the newborn United States, the dollmaking industry in Europe was in full swing. The affluent ordered jointed dolls with kid-leather limbs and glossy composition faces and Paris exported dolls dressed in the latest fashions to teach the rest of the world how to dress. Some of these dolls may have been made for children but there was a definite aura of adulthood and don't-touch about them. The children of the poor certainly didn't have elegant dolls, although more and more of them owned the wooden peg-jointed dolls made by families of Bavarian craftsmen. These simple wooden dolls have been known over the years as peg woodens, Dutch dolls and Flanders babies, but most of them were made in Alpine villages until after the turn of the twentieth century.

European sailors and colonists explored America. European craftsmen explored and developed dollmaking. A few of the commercially made European dolls may have immigrated to the New World during those early centuries, but only one or two of them survived for display in twentieth-century museums. Most colonists, who were trying to combine the civilization of Europe with the survival skills of the Stone Age, made their dolls from whatever was at hand: wood, corn, fruit, nuts, lobster shells, rags and ingenuity.

PART TWO

DOLLS THAT CHILDREN MAKE

SCENES OF NORTH AMERICAN CHILDHOOD

THE NEW WORLD

History is seldom told from a child's point of view. The story of Spanish America is full of tales about treasure found in the New World. French colonial history gives vivid reports of exploration and battle. English settlers left information about crafts and sailing ships, but where were the children?

The children were there. They were there during the first settlements in Acadia, in Virginia, in New Orleans. They moved west with the early wagons into Pennsylvania, Appalachia and the northwest outposts around the Great Lakes. They drove north with the loyalists into Upper Canada and west with all those prairie schooners from Texas to Manitoba.

They may have been left out of the history books because childhood, as we know it, is a relatively modern idea. Our early colonists came from post-medieval cultures that carried many of the traditions of the Middle Ages. Puritan America executed adults and teen-agers for assorted offenses by methods which would horrify any modern court, methods such as pressing a young offender to death with rocks and other heavy weights. By the age of twelve, children were expected to work on an adult scale and defend pioneer forts with their guns. Children were miniaturized adults, in scaled-down adult clothes, doing needed work as the frontiers fanned out.

Limber Jack, Gaspé, Quebec, from
early 1900's (National Museums
of Canada)

Are we to believe then that the children didn't play while all
those major historical events were being recorded? While the French
lost their colonies to the British in 1759? While the British lost their
eastern colonies to the newborn United States during the American
Revolution? That young people didn't play on the Mississippi and
the Detroit River and the Red River, and in the Oregon Territory
from California to British Columbia? You can scour the museums of
the United States and Canada without finding much evidence of
Colonial dolls or toys, but we have paintings and woodcuts of
children at play in Europe during the Middle Ages and a long history
of games and play among the people who settled in North America.

A few families in New England and New France may have had
imported dolls and toys, but how many families were affluent
enough to do that? Most made their dolls from the earth, from corn
and wood and other things, and they returned them to the earth by
the fire or the dump: dolls of corncob and corn husk and apple and
rag and wood.

A WORLD OF TREES

For the first settlers in many areas, the most available material
was wood. From the sea, the New World was an endless dark shadow
of trees. Virgin forests grew dark down to the edge of the water.
People said that a squirrel could walk from tree to tree, without
touching ground, from Quebec to Acadia to Jamestown, and inland
as far as men could go. In Massachussetts, there were gaps in the
forests where the Indians burned the trees down to plant corn,
leaving only stumps behind, but where the corn fields ended, the
trees began again.

To the colonists, the trees were enemies, even though the trees
provided them with material for practically everything they used.
Their houses, furniture, plates, carts and tools were made of wood,
with here and there a piece of leather or forged iron for special
needs. Wood warmed them and built their sailing ships. But the trees

were still enemies. It was necessary to cut them down to clear the way for houses and crops and to keep hostile animals and Indians from the door. Each group of settlers used the trees in a different way. The log cabin, for example, which is an important part of the pioneer story of North America, was not built by New Englanders, because Englishmen did not build log cabins in their native land. The Swedish and German settlers built log cabins but the English built their homes of planks of planed wood.

In the world of a child, food might have been scarce and toys rare, but the trees were always there. A child labored with wood, clearing it and carrying it for fires, but a child could also climb a tree, ride a fallen log or make a doll out of its branches. Dolls of wood, in their simplest form, seem to have been made wherever there were trees. A child needs only the branch of a fallen tree, or a twig, and a cutting tool to make a doll. In the hands of a skilled craftsman, a stump becomes the colorful Kachina doll of the Hopi Indians. The hands of a child have less muscle coordination, but a child can easily make a crude doll with a piece of wood and some corn silk for hair.

A WORLD OF CORN

Corn was the second most available material all over the New World. Colonists labored over it and cursed it. They ate it, slept on its husks and played with it. With it they lived; without it, they might not have survived. It would be perfectly fitting to fly an ear of corn on every North American flagpole, because the continent was literally founded on grains of corn. It was corn that enticed nomadic Indians to stay in one place for the crops, or at least until the fields became barren and forced them to move on. They followed the same pattern as our Stone Age ancestors all over the world, building communities around grain fields and planting the sites of cities. The word "corn" was applied to the long-eared maize first grown in the New World, but according to the *Encyclopedia Brittanica,* the term "corn" is still used all over the world to mean the grain that sustains life in a specific community: wheat in England, oats in Scotland, etc.

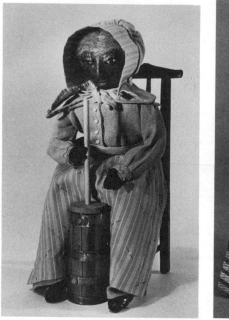

Corn, as North Americans know it, is an indigenous product of this land. The Indians were growing it when the explorers arrived, but it was such a successful food source that it was grown all over Europe within one generation of the first settlers and all over Africa a few generations later.

Corn was a major resource of Colonial life, although most of us wouldn't touch Colonial corn now if we saw it in a supermarket. In the twentieth century we hang red and white multicolored "Indian corn" on our doors, and over our mantle pieces to celebrate autumn, but even that is a healthy descendant of what the colonists dug their teeth into during the seventeenth century. Agriculturists from Virginia say that the Indians had most of the varieties now known, including dent, flint, sweet, and pop corn, but hybridization has given us corn that is long and fat and juicy. Early Indian corn was probably as stubby as those sailors who first said "land ho!" on this side of the Atlantic, a small breed of men if their doorways and the size of their armor is any measure.

In Massachussetts, the Puritans were lucky. They found old corn fields already burned out and abandoned by the Indians, and they found Indians who taught them how to grow corn. Europeans sowed grain by "broadcasting" it across fields in imitation of nature: the wind blew the seeds and the lucky ones grew. The Indians actually planted the seed by placing it in rows of tiny hills. They planted squash and beans and other vegetables on the same slope to enrich the ground, and fertilized the ground by planting a few fish among the crops. The pilgrims in Massachussets did the same; the legend is that they had to tie a dog's foreleg to his neck for forty days after planting so that he wouldn't dig up the fish! Although the children of the time were seen but seldom recorded in the history books, we know that they were living scarecrows in the corn fields, shouting and flapping their arms to scare away the birds.

Colonial children worked with corn, played with corn, supped on corn and went to bed with it. They worked in the corn fields, attended cornhusking bees, ate corn pudding, slept on corn husk mattresses, and when there was time to play in a busy day, they made toys and dolls from corn. They played with circles of corncob. They made corncob houses when they gathered the dried cobs for the fire. And all over the continent, as they followed their parents in wagons into Pennsylvania, over the Alleghenies, into the "northwest" areas around Ohio and Michigan and Upper Canada, and across the prairies to the great mountains, they made corncob dolls.

To tell the story of dollmaking during those early centuries, we must tell the stories of individual families making dolls from available materials in their environment. Scenes of North American Childhood is an attempt to recreate the crude dolls that were made by children during the pioneer years of settlement. The settings described are based on historical research, although the children themselves are fictional.

A CORNCOB DOLL

Abigail held the two corners of her apron high as she carried the pile of dried corncobs from the woodshed to the doorway of the small square house with the peaked roof. The house made an angular silhouette of planed unpainted boards and ruffled roof shingles against the blue sky. She heard the maple tree scraping its spring tracery against the two leather-covered windows, one facing the single downstairs room with its mammoth fireplace, and one facing the upstairs loft where the children slept.

The packed earth under her feet was damp now, with last year's leaves blowing across the spring ground. As she approached the door, Abigail held both corners of the apron in her left hand for a moment so that she could open the door. She slipped one of the corncobs quietly into her apron pocket, then picked up the corners again and entered the house. To Abigail's father, the blackened ceiling beams were just above eye level, but the room looked different to a seven-year-old child. To Abigail, the single U-shaped room, with its arms reaching past either side of the brick fireplace, was an expanse of wide wooden floorboards dotted with silvery square nails. She carried the cobs to her mother, who was stirring dinner over the open flame of the fireplace. Abigail and her mother were dressed exactly alike: dark long-sleeved wool to the floor under a white bodice and long white apron; smooth caps tied under the chin over dark hair.

"Only three of the cobs to fuel the fire, Abigail," her mother said. "There aren't many cobs left now and it's a long way to harvest."

Abigail fingered the small cob in her pocket guiltily as she hurried away to set the table for dinner. The smell of corn pudding was everywhere in the large open part of the room in front of the fire. She could smell it as she took the wooden plates from the sideboard and as she reached into the storage area under the table. She knew that it would follow her to her parents' big bed in the right-hand corner of the room and around the fireplace to the corner where dried apples and flour were stored in a hollowed-out tree

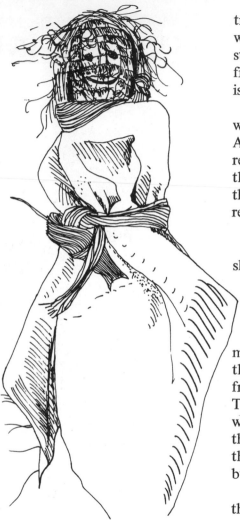

trunk. It would even follow her into the space behind the chimney, where she liked to hide, warm, in the winter. Abigail remembered the strange sight that the chimney had made, standing by itself in the field when the house was being built; when the chimney was finished, the house was built around it.

The black-iron pots, with the handles that burned your hand, were steaming on the brick floor in front of the fireplace now. Abigail backed away to give her mother room and because she remembered too well the day when she had burned her leg on one of those pots. She stretched her arms up in the air, stretching towards the dried herbs hanging on a rod from the ceiling; one day she would reach them, she knew.

"What is in thy pocket, Abigail?"

Abigail snatched her hands down. She pulled the corncob slowly out of her pocket. Her mother looked at her sternly.

"It is only a small one," Abigail said.

A smile twitched at the corner of her mother's mouth.

"Not until thy work is done with the rushes, Abigail."

Abigail nodded. Peeling the rushes. That was the job she hated most. She didn't mind bringing them in from the field, or cleaning the rush holders of grease, but she hated peeling the outside layers from the rushes so that the hard centers could be burned for light. There was still one candle on the blanket chest, but of course candles were too precious for everyday use. They smelled better than rushes though, and they didn't make that oily smoke that drifted around the room when the rushes were soaked in cooking grease and then burned in the iron clamps.

"Dost thee understand, Abigail?" Mother said. "No dolls until thy work is done with the rushes!"

Abigail nodded again. She went to the door to look at the sun. If she hurried with the rushes, there would still be time after dinner to make a corncob doll before dark.

A CORNCOB DOLL

This corncob doll is one of a variety
of simple dolls that can be made from
a cob of corn. The kernels are removed.
Hair and facial features are added.
A scrap dress, hemmed or unhemmed,
completes the doll. Although the
directions are for a fresh cob, a boiled
cob may be used if it is dried a few
days longer than the time specified.
To make a corncob man, simply cut
the cob up the center for 3 inches
from the pointed end to form legs (A).
Another variation, shown here with red
Indian corn, is to leave the kernels on
the cob and sweep the husk up over
the cob to form the head (B). When-
ever you use strips of corn husk to tie
your dolls, use either green husks or
dried husks that have been dampened.

(B)

(A)

MATERIALS FOR
THE CORNCOB DOLL

(See page 138 for discussion of materials and possible substitutions.)
1 whole corncob
Corn silk or frayed 1/4-inch rope
White household glue
Strips of corn husk, string or ribbon
Cloves or peppercorns for features
9- by 12-inch piece of muslin
Optional: the undamaged corn husk
Tools
Small sharp knife
Scissors

(1)

HOW TO MAKE
A CORNCOB DOLL

• *Remove corncob from husk (1)* without damaging husk. Pull back a section of husk from the cob. Remove corn silk from inside the section of husk. Grasp cob and snap it off sharply at the base. Set the undamaged corn husk aside (2).

• *Cut kernels from cob.* Place several thicknesses of newspaper on a table or other hard surface. Grasp cob in one hand, so that pointed end of cob rests on the newspaper. Slice off kernels with a small sharp knife by slicing away from you towards table. When kernels are removed, scrape knife blade back in opposite direction in short strokes to remove kernel pieces still embedded in cob.

(2)

(3)

HOW TO MAKE
A CORN HUSK CRADLE (5)
If you have saved the whole undamaged husk of the corn, smooth it
with your hands into its original
shape and tie the open ends of the
husk with a strip of corn husk.
Separate the husk at the front to
make a place for the doll. The doll's
dress should be removed before
placing the doll in the cradle.

- *Dry cob and husk* in well-lit area
for 3 weeks. Dry the corn silk for hair.
- *Add hair to dried corncob* by glueing strands of corn silk or frayed rope
to the blunt end of the cob (3).
- *To add a scarf,* tie a strip of corn
husk around the cob about 2 inches
from the top of the head to form
a neck.
- *To make a face,* embed cloves or
peppercorns in the kernel holes of the
cob to indicate eyes, nose and mouth.
- *To make a scrap dress,* cut a 1½-
inch slit diagonally in the center of
the square of muslin. Push the cob
through the slit. Gather the dress at
the "waist" and tie with a strip of
corn husk (4).

(4)

(5)

A STUMP DOLL

Ten-year-old Phillippe hurried through the trees toward the river, brushing aside the undergrowth and climbing over fallen logs in his haste. Every few minutes he stopped impatiently to wait for Dominique, whose seven-year-old legs could not keep pace with his. Everyone in the seignuery had heard the news by now. The expedition, which had been gone all summer, was finally returning from the mouth of the Mississippi River. The ships were probably at anchor down the St. Lawrence River. If Phillippe didn't hurry, he would miss the canoes when they landed.

"Hurry up Dominique! Hurry up!"

"But Phillippe, I don't want to go to the river! You promised to make me a doll when you finished your work today. You promised!"

"How many times must I tell you, little fool. The knife is in my pocket. I will make your silly doll when we get to the river."

Dominique was not satisfied, but she had little choice but to follow him.

Phillippe knew that it would be faster to go by the road, but he never walked on the road alone. The Indians had not attacked travelers on the road for many years, but Phillippe could not forget the stories that the old settlers told around the fire at night, stories about Indians leaping out of the trees with a scream of "Casee Koues!"

There was also a chance that he might meet his father and mother on the road. He had not asked permission to leave his work, storing smoked hams and venison, and filling the winter cellars with turnips and carrots and apples. Everyone was going to the river, but there are times when it is best not to take a chance on the wrong answer. The woods were safer on all counts, even if he had to drag Dominique behind him. He had been told to look after Dominique so there was no choice but to bring her along. Sisters, especially little sisters, were always a great nuisance, although he had to admit that Dominique was the one person in the world who really appreciated his wood carvings.

Phillippe had been born near Montreal. He had grown up with the men who went out to explore the land and to fight the British. He had gone to the river to watch every expedition depart: the party that fought in Hudson's Bay and Newfoundland, the men who had followed the D'Ibervilles to Louisiana, and even the group that had gone out to defend the town from an expected Indian attack, which did not occur. When he was younger, Phillippe had wanted to be one of the *couriers des bois',* the fur traders who paddled their canoes out into the great river and came back loaded with furs, but now he knew that he would one day go with an expedition to the settlement in Lousiana.

He saw the towers of the château a few minutes before he burst through the trees to the river. People were gathered along the grassy edge, but there were no boats in sight. He slowed down to catch his breath and to wait for Dominique, who was huffing along behind him, holding her skirt up in the air.

"Wait Phillippe! Wait for me!"

He didn't wait. He moved forward to a spot on a small hill where he could see the canoes as they came around the river bend. By the time his sister joined him, he was whittling away on her doll.

"You see, little baby, I'm making your doll."

"Is it the mama doll?"

"No, Dominique, it's just a stump doll. I'll finish the mama and papa doll for you later today, if you don't tell our mama that we didn't finish the work in the cellar. It will snow soon enough, and mama is usually too busy to smile when it's time for the first snow."

He kept one eye on the doll and one eye on the river as the wood shavings fell on the dying grass and brown leaves at his feet. It would not be a very good doll this time. He could not keep his mind on it. But it was good enough for Dominique, who would probably end up wrapping it in an old scrap of cloth anyway.

A STUMP DOLL

A crude stump doll can be made from any piece of wood. Although the directions call for a tree branch 10 inches long and 2 inches in diameter, the idea can be adapted to any size or shape of wood. A stump with branches attached might be cut to make a doll with arms. The doll becomes a baby when it is wrapped in a scrap blanket. It can also be clothed in a scrap dress. To make the doll, you need only peel off the bark at one end, paint or carve a face and add hair.

MATERIALS FOR
THE STUMP DOLL

(See page 138 for discussion of materials and possible substitutions.)
Piece of a tree branch, about 10 inches
   long and 2 inches in diameter
Watercolors or berry stain
Grass, corn silk or frayed 1/4-inch rope
White household glue or 2 nails
Strip of cloth 12 inches long and
   2 inches wide
Optional: 10-inch square of cloth and
   6-inch length of corn husk or ribbon
Tools
Small sharp knife
Paintbrush
Scissors

HOW TO MAKE A STUMP DOLL

• *Peel the bark* away for 2 inches from the top of the stump of wood. The peeled portion will be moist. It can be used immediately or dried for about 2 days.

• *To make features,* paint or carve eyes, nose and mouth.

• *Attach hair* by glueing or nailing strands of grass, corn silk or frayed rope to the top of the stump. The rope shown in the photograph was attached to the wood at the top center of the head, unraveled and crossed over the top of the head to give height, and tied down with a scarf.

• *To add the scarf,* wrap the 12-inch strip of cloth across the hair, cross it at the back of the doll and tie it at the front where the peeled and unpeeled wood meet. Tie the ends to make a scarf.

• *To make the dress,* cut a 3-inch slit in the center of the square of cloth. Insert the stump through the hole in the cloth. Tie the dress at the neck scarf with a piece of corn husk or ribbon. Pull some of the material up above the ribbon to form a bodice.

A TWIG DOLL

A soldier of the Continental army scrambled through stark winter trees toward the farmhouse on the hill. It was the winter of Valley Forge. He was cold and he was hungry. Only an accident of war had brought him close enough to the farm to sneak home for a few hours. As he topped the rise, he saw his daughter, Sarah, carrying the milk, and a few apples in her apron, from the barn to the house. He didn't call out. Not yet. He wanted to look around him for just a few solitary moments to savor the farm alone. He and his wife had built the house and the barn by hand, carrying one stone after another from the riverbed below.

He climbed the hill to the barn where the brown and white milk cow rubbed her flank against the wall. The soldier rubbed the cow's head tenderly, and then moved to the secret partition where the winter supplies were kept. As he suspected, there were only a few bags of grain, most of it seed grain, and a small store of apples. He smiled as he remembered the winter when he had come close, for the only time, to striking his wife; she had wanted to bake bread from the seed grain, but families that eat the seed grain have nothing to plant in the spring.

He went out of the barn and down the slope to the house. Through the window he could see the boys sitting at the large wooden table. His wife was stirring porridge over the open flame of the fireplace. As he watched, she reached for salt from the wooden box on the stone mantle. The house had only a single room with a ladder to the second-story loft. What was his daughter Sarah doing in the corner? She had a small pile of sticks and a rag. Suddenly he realized that she was making a doll. Not a fine rag doll like the ones that Sarah and her mother had made in other years. What on earth was left in this winter place to make dolls for a little girl? The apples were too precious. The corn was gone. There should be husks, but maybe things were bad enough to save even the husks for soup, the kind that the Indians once made in long, cold winters. As he moved towards the door, with a picture of Sarah and her few twigs in his

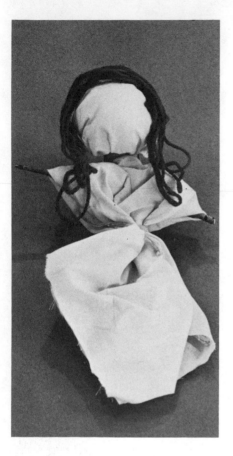

head, the soldier fingered the knife he carried in his pocket. He forgot for a moment that he was looking for warmth and food. He only had a few hours, but maybe he could carve a small doll for the girl, something to keep her happy until he returned in the spring. If he returned in the spring. It was better not to think about that now.

The soldier slowly opened the door. "I'm home," he called. "I'm home."

A TWIG DOLL

This doll was made from the thin end of a living tree branch. It could also be made with dried twigs or with larger sticks. Two twigs are crossed and tied to form a body. The body can also be made of wire or wrapped with strips of cloth as shown in the section on applehead dolls. Cotton balls wrapped in muslin are attached for a head, which can be decorated with hair and facial features. The doll is then wrapped in a scrap dress.

MATERIALS FOR
THE TWIG DOLL

(See page 138 for discussion of materials and possible substitutions.)
Straight twig, 8 inches long
Forked twig, 10 inches long and
   1/4 inch in diameter
Strips of corn husk
4 cotton balls
4-inch square of muslin
10-inch square of muslin
10-inch length of ribbon
Lengths of 1/4-inch rope or yarn
Cloth patches of contrasting colors
White household glue
Tools
Needle and thread
Scissors

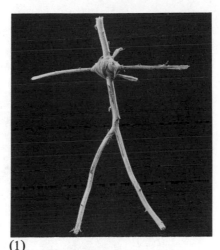

(1)

HOW TO MAKE A TWIG DOLL

• *Cross the 2 twigs (1).* Position the 8-inch twig approximately 1 inch from the unforked end of the 10-inch twig. Tie the twigs with about 3 strips of damp corn husk where they cross. Wrap the strips around the twigs several times to secure them as tightly as possible. The husk will tighten as it dries.

• *To make the doll's head,* cover the cotton balls with the 4-inch square of muslin. Position the cotton in the center of the cloth and fluff the cotton out so that the head will have a soft, rounded appearance. Gather together the 4 corners of the square. Smooth one side as much as possible for the face, with all excess gathering in the back.

• *Attach the head to the body (2),* by inserting the top of the crossed twigs into the cotton stuffing of the head.

• *Tie the head to the crossed twigs* with a corn husk strip. Adjust the strip so that the muslin is stretched as smoothly as possible over the cotton balls.

• *Dress the doll.* Cut a slit the diameter of the head, approximately 3 inches, in the center of the 10-inch square of muslin. Insert the head through slit. Fold raw edges under at each sleeve, so that they are proportionate to the doll's arms. Adjust the dress by fluffing and smoothing folds and wrinkles. Tie at the waist with the ribbon.

• *To add the hair,* sew 3 lengths of rope or several strands of yarn to top of head. Fray the rope, or separate the yarn, and braid.

• *To add features,* cut eyes, nose and mouth out of cloth patches and glue to face.

(2)

51

A GRASS DOLL

The two Conestoga wagons made strange dark shapes against the twilight sky. The Fraser and the Heimrich families were unusually quiet as they packed away the last of the knives they had used for supper. It would be their last supper together. The Frasers were going south, over the Allegheny Mountains to settle in the mountain country beyond. The Heimrich family was moving north, into Upper Canada.

The two families had been neighbors for many years, but they were careful on this last night to talk only about memories and not about the war. They remembered too well the arguments that had nearly shattered their friendship when the Heimrichs announced that they would follow the loyalists into British territory in Canada. There were too many years of common struggle behind them to part as anything but friends.

The children of both families were restless tonight, but not yet ready to sleep. They knew that they were saying goodbye to one another, but they didn't really understand why. Mrs. Heimrich and Mrs. Fraser sat on the grass together, watching the light fade while the two girls pulled the long grass from the field and wrapped it together into a family of dolls. They had made two mothers and two fathers which they placed together in a circle. It was a sad reminder of their last night together.

The two families would start the next day in opposite directions. It would be a long walk for both of them, because only the smallest children could ride in the wagon. The Conestoga wagon was an adaption of a German wagon, redesigned by Pennsylvania immigrants to carry heavy loads over the difficult roads of the New World. As Mr. Heimrich said often enough, it was an overstatement to call them roads. They were Indian trails, widened and beaten down by the military expeditions, and dotted with stumps. The roads were heavily rutted by the traffic that had trundled along them, but there was no doubt that the Conestoga wagons were the only vehicles that could haul heavy loads of goods over the mountains. Travel was

steady enough even if the whole family had to walk, at least until the wagon stranded itself on a stump. People were already using a new phrase, "It's got me stumped!"

"It's time, children," Mrs. Fraser said. The children were reluctant, even though the sun was nearly down, but with a little urging they gathered their dolls and followed their mothers to the place where they would sleep. None of them spoke of the long journey ahead. Both families had pioneered the land once already, and it was better not to think too much in advance of what it would be like to start again after they reached their destinations.

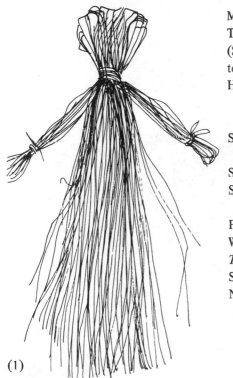

(1)

A GRASS DOLL

A crude temporary doll can be made from green grass. A more permanent doll will result from dried grass, raffia or dried corn husks, all of which should be sprayed with a solution of 2 tablespoons of glycerine in a quart of water to make them flexible. You will fold the long strips, stuff the fold with extra material and tie to form a head, and then turn back a few pieces of grass or husk on each side for arms. Hair and facial features are then added. This doll can be very attractive when dressed like the raffia doll on page 52.

MATERIALS FOR THE GRASS DOLL

(See page 138 for discussion of materials and possible substitutions.)
Handful of 24-inch-long grass, either green or dried, or shorter strips of corn husk (or raffia)
Strips of grass or corn husk to stuff head
Strips of grass or corn husk for ties
Several 8-inch-long strands of grass or corn husk for braids
Felt scraps
White household glue
Tools
Scissors
Needle and thread

HOW TO MAKE A GRASS DOLL

• *To make the body (1),* smooth the grass or husks into long even strands. Fold the bundle of strands in the middle. Stuff the center fold with the extra pieces of grass or husk and tie at the neck to form a head. If the grass you use is too fragile to make a strong tie, use string.

• *To make the arms,* separate out about 10 strands of grass or husk from each side of the body. Clip the ends of the separated strands to make them even. Fold back the strands 2 inches and tie 1 inch from the fold to form hands.

• *To make the braided hair (2),* smooth out the 8-inch strands. Tie the bundle at one end. Braid the strands and tie at the other end. Sew braid to head.

• *Make a face* by cutting felt to form features and glueing pieces to the head.

• *Trim the skirt* at the hem with scissors to make it even.

(2)

A WOODEN SPOON DOLL
A CLOTHES PEG DOLL

It was her second day in the new village. Anna felt as if she had been walking all her life beside the shaggy velvet-brown fur of the oxen which pulled their wagon to Upper Canada. It was only a few weeks, but it felt like a much longer time over bumpy grass hills and high rocks to this village where her cousins lived. She had walked around the village once with her parents: to the wheelwright, who replaced the metal rims rubbed through on the new corduroy roads; to the tannery, where the smell of tanned leather overwhelmed you in a room literally tapestried with leather; to the general store, which was the center of everything here as it had been in the village she had left behind her. For reasons she didn't understand, she was lonelier staying with her cousin in this new village than she had been during all the long weeks on the trail.

All of the other women and girls in the house were working. Her cousin, Maria, was kneading bread on a board at the table in front of the fire. Anna's mother and aunt were in the barn tossing the wheat in a blanket, to separate the chaff. Anna had started to help, after they had unpacked the wagon, but her mother had looked at her a long time and then said, "Anna, today you can rest. You look very tired."

"Resting" was all right, as long as you were doing something. Anna had rested all afternoon in the house, tying and untying hanky dolls from scraps of cloth left over from the quilting, but she wished now that she had something with which to make a real doll. She got up and began walking around the room, touching things with her fingers. She could smell the carrots and potatoes and meat cooking in the iron pot over the fireplace flame. She could smell the herb garden through the open door. Through the window she could see the pigs eating from a pile of rotting apples gathered from the orchard. Beyond the pigs, a road ran past the white picket fence that surrounded the house.

Anna picked up a wooden spoon that had been left on the table. Deftly she arranged a piece of cloth on the spoon to form a doll. It was her aunt's spoon, so she could not make a face on it, but it was a nice feeling to hold the doll even though she knew it was temporary. Anna clutched the doll and walked across the room to the window. She could see her mother and father and her aunts and uncles and cousins busy around the barn, but for the moment she was glad that she was "resting." With the small doll in her hand, it was less lonely than it had seemed before in this new place she would somehow learn to call home. She began to look around the room for other things that she could make into dolls, a darning egg, perhaps, or even a clothes peg.

57

A WOODEN SPOON DOLL

Children can make simple dolls from a variety of household items. If the item has been discarded, the doll-maker may paint it or carve it, but if the item is still in use, the dollmaker can still use it temporarily. A wooden spoon doll is merely a spoon, with a painted face, in a scrap dress. Exactly the same doll can be made from a piece of driftwood, or any interesting piece of wood.

MATERIALS FOR
THE WOODEN SPOON DOLL

(See page 138 for discussion of materials and possible substitutions.)

1 wooden spoon
Watercolors or berry stain
12-inch square of cloth
Strip of cloth, 15 inches long and
    2 inches wide
Tools
Paintbrush
Small sharp knife
Scissors
Optional: needle and thread

HOW TO MAKE
A WOODEN SPOON DOLL

• *Paint or carve features and hair* on the smooth rounded back of the spoon bowl.

• *Dress the doll.* Cut a straight 1-inch slit in the center of the square of cloth. Insert the spoon handle through the slit. Fold raw edges of cloth under to make a smooth edge. You may prefer to iron or sew edges flat. Tie the dress at the waist by wrapping the 15-inch strip of cloth several times around the "waist" and tying at the back. Fluff the skirt material to suggest the shape of a bodice and skirt.

A CLOTHES PEG DOLL

Nineteenth-century clothes pegs had the rounded, flat-sided heads shown in this doll (2). To use modern pegs, choose those that are slit only part way to the head, so that there is enough room on the peg to make a face. Note the two pegs in photo and the choice of either wire or pipe cleaner for arms (1).

(1)

MATERIALS FOR
THE CLOTHES PEG DOLL

(See page 138 for discussion of materials and possible substitutions.)
1 clothes peg
6-inch length of 20-gauge black wire or 1 pipe cleaner
Watercolors or berry stain
Two 2-inch lengths of twine or one 2-inch length of 1/4-inch rope
White household glue
6-inch square of cloth
6-inch length of wool or string
Tools
Small sharp knife
Paintbrush
Scissors

(2)

HOW TO MAKE
A CLOTHES PEG DOLL

• *To make the arms (1),* wind wire or pipe cleaner around the body of the peg once, leaving equal amounts extending on either side. If wire slips, groove the side of peg slightly to hold. Bend arms at shoulders and elbows.

• *To make the face,* paint eyes, nose and mouth on the head of the clothes peg.

• *To add the hair,* separate strands of twine or rope. Fold sharply in half. Apply glue at fold and attach to the head of the peg, pressing with fingers against top and side of head until glue dries.

• *Dress the doll.* Make a 1-inch slit in the center of the cloth square and insert the peg through the slit. Tie at the "waist" with the length of wool or string, being sure to cover the wire wrapped around the peg. Fluff material to suggest a dress.

A DARNING EGG DOLL

Bessie Mae ran down the path toward the river, pausing only long enough to look back at the house. The sheets were blowing back and forth in front of the house, but there was nobody in sight. Papa and Mama were working in the garden behind the house and there would be trouble if they found her out of bed when she still had the measles spots, but Bessie Mae had made up her mind so there was no stopping. She was nine years old now, so she was grown up.

Bessie Mae had been hiding the old darning egg in the shed by the river for three weeks, because she knew that Mama would have the baby soon.

Bessie Mae ducked through the trees, and pulled back quick, but it was too late. Uncle Zack had seen her.

"Hey there, black girl. What are you doing out of bed?"

"My name's not black girl, it's Bessie Mae!"

Uncle Zack just laughed from his perch on the edge of the river bank. He only did it to make her mad. She always said that she wasn't going to mind, but she always got mad. Always.

"Shush, Uncle Zack. Don't tell!"

Bessie Mae stopped inside the shed door to adjust her eyes to the dark. There was a bucket near the corner; it had been there all summer. When her eyes picked it out, she moved quickly along the inside wall. She stopped at the sound of her father's voice.

"Who you talking to, Zack?" her father said.

"Nobody!" Uncle Zack said.

"I heard you talking. Who you talking to?"

"Aw, I was talking to myself. A man got a right to talk to himself if he wants to."

Bessie Mae held her breath as her father came through the door of the shed. She had stepped into the dark shadow in the corner, but if he turned his head he'd see her.

Papa dumped the stack of wood on the shed floor and walked out humming to himself. Bessie Mae knew that she had taken enough chances for one day. She plucked the darning egg out from

under the bucket and tiptoed to the door. She had found the darning egg in a field, covered with mud, and had known at once that it would be a perfect gift for her mama. It was scrubbed now, and polished. The painted face was dry. As soon as she cut out the two pieces of material for clothes, she would have a doll that would make Mama laugh. Bessie Mae took a deep breath and ran back up the path towards the house, rubbing the shiny surface of the darning egg as she dodged across the field of grass.

(1)

A DARNING EGG DOLL

An old-fashioned darning egg is inserted in the heel of a sock while darning a hole. It is only one of a variety of household items that can be used for this simple doll. (Use a wooden-handled bell, for example, marking the top of the handle for a face.) The doll is nothing more than a face peeping out between a hat and a dress, but it delights a child.

MATERIALS FOR
THE DARNING EGG DOLL

(See page 138 for discussion of materials and possible substitutions.)
1 darning egg
Watercolors or berry stain
8-inch square of cloth
Length of yarn
4-inch square of cloth
Tools
Scissors
Paintbrush

HOW TO MAKE A
A DARNING EGG DOLL

- *Paint a face* on the rounded front of the darning egg.
- *Make a scrap dress (1)* by cutting a slit in the 8-inch square of cloth and inserting the darning egg through the slit. Tie a piece of yarn around the neck of the dress so that a ruffled edge stands up.
- *Make a scrap hat (2)* from the 4-inch square of cloth. Fold the square twice to form a 2-inch square. Clip the folded corner off the square with scissors, cutting 1/2 inch down from corner on both sides. Open square. Round the edges to make a circle. Pull down on doll's head.

(2)

HANKY PANKY FAMILY

Three of the children hung out of the back of the wagon, watching the prairie grass recede in puffs of dust around the cow that was tied behind. When they turned forward, the children could see the soft-brimmed hat of their brother John and the bonnet brim of their mother outlined against the blue sky through the arched front of the wagon. Papa was just a sun hazed blur between the horses on the prairie ahead, his arms outstretched to pull the two horses along.

The girls wore white aprons, now soiled, over their printed long-sleeved dresses. Their hair, combed at dawn, straggled out now beneath their bonnets. The youngest one, Susannah, was the grubbiest in her yellow dress, but she was more concerned about the yellow dress on her doll, Little Susannah. The girls had all made dolls during the long days on the wagon train, when the grass was a green carpet puddled with spring, and when the grass turned stubbly brown under a sun so hot that Pa said it could fry the chickens crated against the side of the wagon.

Susannah was restless and hungry. She knew better than to talk about food because dried beef and biscuits didn't taste like food anyway.

"Mama, Susannah won't stop fidgeting and whining!"

Their mother's bonnet turned toward them. "Mathilda. Do you remember the corn husks I wrapped up when we stopped last?"

"Yes, Mama."

"Get them out Mathilda. We can make Susannah a doll."

"We used it already Mama. Don't you remember, you made Susannah a doll with them already."

She could hear Mama sigh at the front of the wagon.

"What about the hankies Mama! You promised to show us how to make hanky dolls. Don't you remember?"

"Of course I do Mathilda. Don't shout! I can hear you. Well then, if you can find the clean hankies without disturbing the rest of the clothes, bring them to me. Susannah. Stop fussing and come up here. Mama is going to make you the Hanky Panky Family."

THE HANKY PANKY FAMILY

These dolls can be made anywhere. A Kentucky mother made one for her daughter on those Sunday mornings when the little girl was restless in church. One handkerchief will make a doll that can be untied later, leaving the hanky intact. Four hankies make a family.

MATERIALS FOR THE HANKY PANKY FAMILY

2 large men's handkerchiefs
2 small ladies' handkerchiefs

(1)

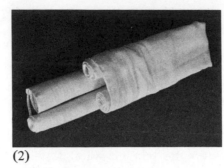

(2)

HOW TO MAKE THE HANKY PANKY FAMILY

To Make the Papa or Mama Doll

• *Lay a large hanky flat* on the table, or on your lap. Carefully roll one edge towards the middle (1). Roll the opposite edge towards the middle.

• *Fold 1/3 of the rolled hanky over (2),* so that 1/3 of the rolls still show. Carefully turn the rolled hanky over.

(3)

• *Ease out the short edges (3),* which are now on the bottom. Roll the short edge up a little and tie the two ends around the rolled hanky. Pull out the "face" and straighten the "arms." When the doll is turned so that the rolls show (4), you have a papa doll with trousers. Turn the doll over and you have a mama doll in a long skirt (5).

(4)

66

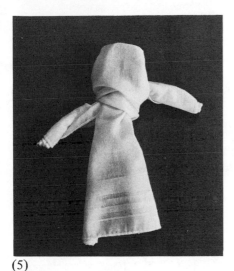

(5)

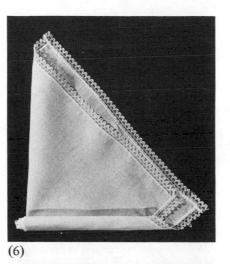

(6)

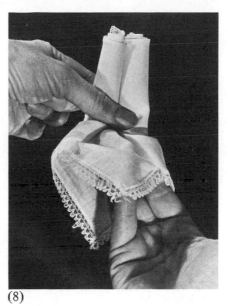

(8)

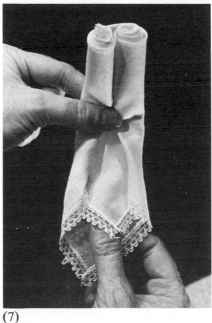

(7)

To Make the Child Doll
• *Lay one of the short hankies flat* on the table and proceed as you would for the mama and papa doll.

To Make Twins in a Cradle
• *Lay a small hanky flat* on the table. Fold it corner to corner to make a triangle. Roll one corner towards the center (6). Roll opposite corner towards the center. The top half of these rolls will eventually become the twins.

• *Hold the rolled hanky with the pointed end down (7).* The next step is a difficult one. Your goal is to pull the inside pointed layer forward to form the front of the cradle, and the outside or back pointed layer backward to form the back of the cradle. Begin by spreading the fingers of one hand between the 2 layers (8).

(9)

• *Pull the pointed end of the back layer up (9),* so that it covers the rolls on the other side.

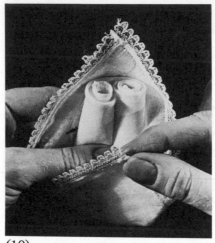

(10)

• *Pull the pointed end of the front layer up (10),* so that it covers the 2 rolls.

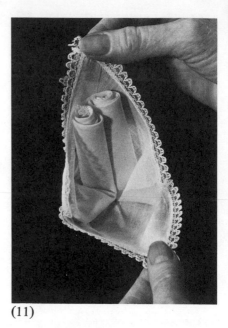

(11)

• *Shape the cradle* by inserting your index finger between rolls and outer layers and smoothing folds. If you hold the 2 points of this hanky, you should have a cradle with 2 rolled "babies" inside (11). The cradle will rock.

PART THREE

DOLLS THAT ADULTS MAKE

DOLLS OF UPPER AND LOWER CANADA

There is an important difference between the dolls that children make and the dolls that adults make. A child projects his imagination onto an object, creating toys that adults cannot see. A box becomes a sailing ship. A stick, a stone or a piece of wood becomes a doll. A child needs only a prop; his imagination does the rest. An adult, on the other hand, makes toys by recreating familiar objects in the adult world. In the seventeenth and eighteenth centuries, adults collected exquisite miniatures that were the prototypes of the realistic toys sold in twentieth-century stores; modern children may clamor for these realistic toys but they continue to make their own fantasy world out of available materials, such as a wooden box or a sand pile.

Adults who made homemade dolls for their children during the last four centuries of North American history also made their dolls out of available materials in the environment, but they used sophisticated adult skills in their craft. The dolls that adults made had realistic limbs, embroidered faces and the clothing style of their period. Their dolls tell a story about the time in which they lived.

THE PERCY BAND COLLECTION

(1)

Part of that historical story can be read in the Percy Band Collection, accumulated by the great-great grandchild of Ezekial Band, who emigrated after the American Revolution from Connecticut to present-day Ontario. Band was one of at least 50,000 loyalists who emigrated to the northern British colonies after the United States declared its independence: roughly 30,000 to Nova Scotia, 7,000 to Quebec and 10,000 to what is now Ontario. These emigrants were primarily British settlers loyal to the crown, and the settlers known as Pennsylvania Deutsch: a combination of Protestant Lutherans, Huguenots and Mennonites from France, Germany and Switzerland, who had come to the New World to escape religious persecution. The "Canada," which for 200 years had been French Quebec and its outposts along the Great Lakes, was divided into Lower Canada (Quebec) and Upper Canada (Ontario), the latter creating a major section of English-speaking settlers in Canada for the first time. The land to the west, beyond the Mississippi and the Great Lakes, was still wilderness.

The Canadian dolls that have survived to reach the shelves of museums have done so primarily because of the Percy Band Collection, now held by Black Creek Pioneer Village, under the Metropolitan Toronto and Region Conservation Authority. The collection has a specific focus: to show the toys that Canadian children played with in the nineteenth century.

One of the historical highlights of the collection is a crèche doll (1), which reflects the French culture in which it was made in Quebec in 1770. The doll is made with a carved beeswax head on a body of rushes, and wears an eighteenth-century French peasant dress. The collection also includes a carved wooden milk cart driven by a French farmer (2). It was carved in 1889 and represents the simple but effective wood carvings that have been part of French-Canadian folk art for centuries.

(2)

Wood is a primary environmental material in Quebec. Although early French settlers grew many crops, their pioneer economy was based on the trees, and the furs that were trapped in the forest, rather than on the agricultural and small craft industries that were the base of the British colonies of that time in Massachusetts and Virginia. A folk art based on crafted wood goes back as far as 1670, when Quebec City imported twenty craftsmen from France to start its first furniture school. Designs followed the latest furniture fashions of France until 1759, when communication between Quebec and France was terminated by the British victory over the French in North America. The Louis IV styles then popular in France remained the prevalent style in furniture and woodcraft in Quebec and have established themselves firmly as French-Canadian folk art.

When the loyalists migrated to Canada after the American Revolution they introduced the folk art of Britain and other parts of Europe. This carved Judy doll (3), typical of the Punch and Judy dolls that delighted children in Europe and America, was carved in 1785 and carried to Upper Canada, now Ontario, by Ezekial Band, the loyalist ancestor of twentieth-century doll collector Percy Band.

(3)

73

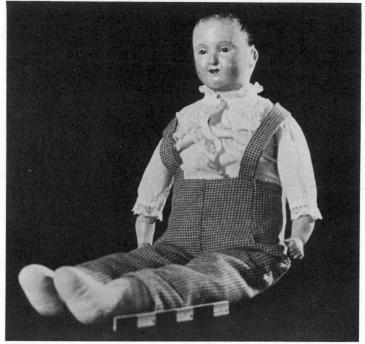

(5)

The Percy Band Collection was started with the Annie Cooley doll, made in 1840 (4). It was followed by many handmade Canadian dolls, including the rare boy doll (5) with a papier-mâché head and stuffed body who is dressed in brown-and-white-checked trousers and a white shirt. The doll belonged to Josephine Langlois, daughter of John Sandfield Macdonald, the first Premier of the Province of Ontario.

Although china heads were not made in North America, they can be included in a discussion of North American dolls because the heads, imported from Europe, were attached to the bodies of dolls that were stuffed and dressed at home. A good example is the china head (6) bought by a Canadian in Brantford, Ontario, in 1870 for seventy-five cents.

A homemade doll with a store-bought head (7) is a typical example of the stuffed bodies usually made at home in both the United States and Canada; most of these dolls have bodies that are disproportionate in size to the head. China-head dolls often depicted

(4)

Lobster Doll (National Museums of Canada)

(7)

(6)

(9)

(10)

(8)

professional people admired by women and young girls, as shown in the three nursing dolls (8, 9, 10) clothed in the particular costumes of the hospitals in which they worked.

The interest in dolls, in both the United States and Canada, was greatly stimulated by the doll collection started by the young Princess Victoria at age fourteen and known to the world throughout Queen Victoria's long reign. Until the Victorian era, most dolls had brown eyes, but Queen Victoria's eyes were blue, so most dolls now have blue eyes. Victoria chose wooden dolls, although the European fashion rage of the time was for wax, composition and Parian dolls. Thirty-two of the princess' dolls were dressed by her, and the rest were dressed by her governess, the Baroness Lehzen. The dolls represent famous artists dressed for their roles in the ballet or opera; they also represent court ladies.

CANADIAN FRONTIER DOLLS

The courtiers of Queen Victoria's collection are at the opposite end of the spectrum from the simple homemade dolls found in other

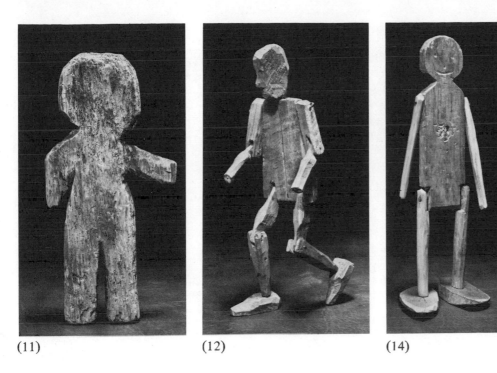

(11) (12) (14)

(13)

Canadian collections. The Canadian Center for Folk Culture Studies, which is part of the National Museum of Man in Ottawa, owns several crudely carved wooden dolls (11) which are probably typical of dolls made by inexperienced hands in both the United States and Canada. Some of these wooden dolls were carved in the twentieth century, modern but still primitive versions of the French-Canadian wood carvings that were made at the beginning of Canadian doll history.

One of the oldest wooden folk dolls, a type that remained popular into the twentieth century, is a loose-limbed doll variously known as a Limber Jack or a Dancing Dan. This doll is either supported on a stick or attached to a separate board; in either case, the owner makes the doll dance with a wild clattering of wooden feet. These Limber Jacks made in the early twentieth century in Gaspé, Quebec (12), and Shelburne County, Nova Scotia (13), are made on exactly the same principle as the dancing doll made in 1940 in Orillia, Ontario (14).

77

(15)

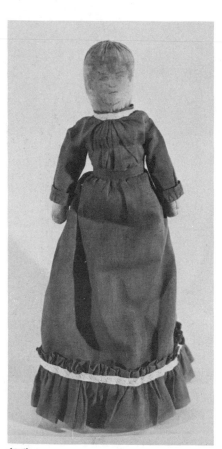

(16)

(17)

UPPER CANADA

The dolls of Quebec are part of a tradition that goes back to nineteenth-century Lower Canada and, before that, to New France. The dolls of Ontario, or Upper Canada, usually reflect the English-speaking part of Canada, the part settled after the American Revolution by loyalists.

The wooden gentleman doll (15), probably of white pine, was made by William Henry McDonald for his daughter Amy. Mr. McDonald, who liked to sketch and carve for pleasure, finished Peter Jimmy, as this doll was named, late on Christmas Eve of 1898. He intended to paint the doll later, but Miss McDonald declared that she loved him just the way he was, and so he has retained his natural wood finish. The doll is articulated at the shoulders and hips, with a riveted iron nail and copper rivets.

Miss McDonald's grandmother, Mrs. J. Cadman, created "Ruth," the cotton doll (16), stuffed with old cotton, in 1900. Mr. McDonald designed the facial features, which had to be re-inked each time the doll was washed. This doll, which was Miss McDonald's

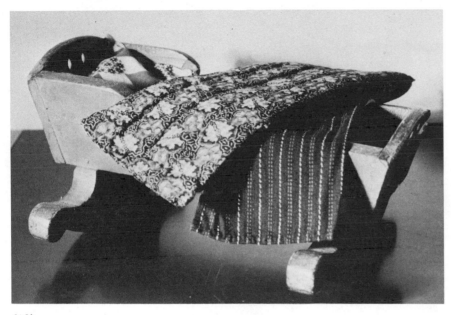

(18)

favorite, originally came dressed in a flannelette nightdress, but Miss McDonald's sister soon created the fashionable red dress of the period. The matching hat is missing. The doll is also wearing white cotton drawers, trimmed with eyelet edging.

An important part of the tradition of Upper Canada was contributed by the Mennonites who settled near Kitchener, Ontario. The doll made by Leah Reist Martin for Salome Martin sometime between 1902 and 1908 is a homemade stuffed body with a store-bought china head (17). It could easily have rested in the handmade cradle (18), complete with straw-stuffed tick, pillow and sheet, comforter and pillowcase from the Swiss-German Mennonite community of the late nineteenth century. A rag doll (19), from the same part of Waterloo County, was probably made in the early twentieth century.

By that time Upper and Lower Canada were no longer on the map, their names replaced by the name "Canada" when the two territories were joined by the Confederation of 1867. Canadians were moving west across the prairies, making paper dolls out of Eaton's catalogues in sod houses on the plains, and moving with the railway tracks across the mountains to the Pacific.

(19)

THE INDEX OF AMERICAN DESIGN

THE UNITED STATES

Who is Catherine Deshler? The only thing we know about her is that she was the daughter of a French Huguenot refugee, and that she owned a doll that may have been made as early as 1683. The doll survives, but nothing else about Catherine Deshler is known to us. We know something about French Huguenots in Europe in the seventeenth century, however; they were trapped in the continual revolt-and-repression of Protestant religious rebels on a continent committed to the Papal Church. Like many of America's early settlers, the Deshlers probably came to the New World to enjoy religious freedom.

Is it important to know the story of Catherine Deshler? She was just one of thousands of human beings who makes up the story of America. Was her doll worth keeping? In its own day it was an everyday object; today it is folk art. We seldom value our artists and craftsmen so most of that folk art is gone forever, but thanks to a wise decision during the Great Depression of the 1930's, a few dozen dolls from museums around the United States were recorded in the Index of American Design at the National Gallery of Art in Washington, D.C.

(2)

(3)

(1)

THE INDEX OF AMERICAN DESIGN

The Index of American Design was a Federal Art Project of the Works Progress Administration, commonly known as the W.P.A. The aim of the Index was to compile material for a nationwide pictorial survey of design in the American decorative, useful and folk arts from their inception to about 1890. Artists were sent to museums and collectors throughout the country to make accurate paintings of American decorative arts, including Early American handmade dolls. Slides of these dolls, as well as of commercial dolls, are available on a library loan basis from the National Gallery of Art.

These are dolls of wood and cloth and corn husk and nuts, dolls made by mountain folk and townspeople from Massachusetts and Kentucky to Arizona and California. There are Indians depicted by settlers and settlers depicted by Indians, snatches of history in dolls kept by great-great-grandchildren and dolls found in war. The oldest doll (page 80), assumed to be made in America, is the doll that belonged to Catherine Deshler. There were two of these dolls once, but the second one is believed to have been broken or lost during the Columbian Exposition in 1893.

The Deshler doll is a small reminder of the early French settlers in North America. Another doll, made a century later in 1795, gives us a brief look at the world of the Spanish in America, who explored from Florida through Mexico and the southern mountain states of the present-day United States to California. This doll (1) was made by an Indian woman to depict her vision of white settlers on San Miguel, one of the Santa Barbara Islands. San Miguel was explored by the Spanish in the sixteenth century, and settled by farmers until the middle of the nineteenth century, when the overgrazed land was given back to nature.

All of the dolls pictured in the Index have backgrounds shrouded in mystery. Their genealogy is contained in memories passed down from generation to generation:

"My grandmother said that her mother played with this doll as a child. . . ."

"The antique dealer was told it came from this area. . . ."

"The man I bought it from told me that it was made. . . ."

WOODEN DOLLS

Although the old dolls in this collection were crafted by adult hands, they were made of the same environmental materials used in the crude dolls made by children. Wood was the staple material of both royal dolls and peasant dolls in medieval times, and many of the nineteenth-century dolls are also made of wood. This cheerful little doll (2) has been verified by the great-grandson of the original owner as being made in the eighteenth century. It is painted wood, dressed in blue silk and an apron of stiff calico. Many of the early dolls were carved of a single block of wood, like the doll (3) made for a little girl called Elsie Bentley. The doll was cut from a block of walnut about 1805 and wears a gingham dress. But sometimes even the dress was made of wood, as it was in the doll (4) carved in the early nineteenth century by a Swiss dollmaker in New Hampshire.

(4)

(5)

Who was Elsie Bentley? Who was the Swiss dollmaker in New Hampshire, who so lovingly carved a block of wood? Was this a mountain craft imported into America? Was the Swiss doll made from a tree that was warmed and weathered in wind and rain outside somebody's kitchen door? Why don't we know more about the lives of the people who made these dolls? Although there were diaries, few were written by women in the early centuries of American life. Those few diaries were most often kept by the affluent and the educated, who seldom mentioned dolls. Records of ordinary people, who made ordinary homemade dolls, are very scarce.

The nineteenth century was a century of mechanization in America. It was the age of the mechanized plow and the horseless carriage, an age when things began to move without human hands. Mechanical dolls were 50 years in the future when this wooden doll (5) was carved and painted in some unknown corner of America in 1800, but the jointed limbs reflect an effort to make dolls move, an effort that had gone on since ancient Greek and Roman days. The simplest kind of jointed dolls had wooden arms and legs attached to a wooden body with wooden pegs. The doll in photograph 6 shows, step by step, what a creative homemaker could make from such a simple doll.

Dollmakers often used wood for the only part of a dressed doll that shows, the head. Even when Parisian artisans made extravagantly dressed dolls for royal children in the seventeenth and eighteenth centuries, the bodies were nothing more than pouches filled with sawdust. The doll that was made at home for an American called Peggy Barton in 1840 had a wooden head, stump legs, cloth arms and a cotton wig (7). It is an excellent example of an ingenious people using available materials from the environment to fill a specific need. Another good example is the lady with a wooden head and a stylishly sashed costume of white petticoat embroidery (8). The black arms were made by covering the stuffed body with black sateen. This doll is also believed to have been made at home for a child.

(8)

(7)

(6)

85

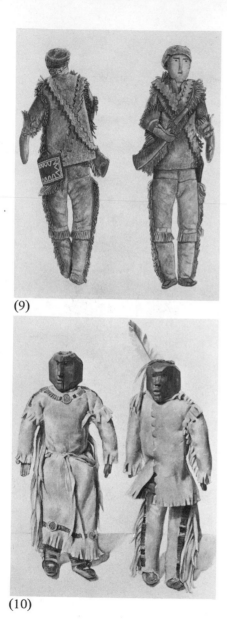

(9)

(10)

DOLLS THAT MIRROR HISTORY

By the middle of the nineteenth century, the great immigration of settlers from Europe was beginning to pour through the seaports of the United States and across the Great Plains. Plains Indians, who were being torn from their traditional cultural roots, met face to face with Europeans, who were also being torn from their cultural roots. What did they see? American Indians have shown us their image of settlers and pioneers, as the Plains Indians did when they made their "frontiersman" (9) in buckskin clothes about 1850. A wig of buffalo skin once covered his head. This doll shows us the type of costume worn by both Indians and pioneer settlers on the frontier in the mid-nineteenth century. Indians also told their own story, as Marie Rose of the Montana Cree Reservation did when she made this pair of Crees (10) in the late nineteenth century.

While the great migration moved east to west, another great drama was being played out on the Civil War battlefields of the North and South. Dolls would seem to be very remote from the battlefields of war, but a Union soldier found this rag doll (11) on a Southern plantation during the Civil War and carried it as a good luck charm until he was safely home.

Dolls have played some peculiar roles during wartimes. "Fashion dolls," which carried the latest women's fashions from Paris to the rest of Europe in the seventeenth and eighteenth centuries, were in such demand by European women that they were often allowed through naval blockades during wartime. War or no war, women wanted to know what was being worn in the fashion capital of the world. An English doll in the collection of "Papier-Mâché, Wax and Mechanical Dolls" at the Index of American Design, is known to have passed through a naval blockade off South Carolina, in 1864, during the American Civil War. Toys were so scarce in the South that the doll became a curiosity. Nina, another doll in the same collection, smuggled morphine and quinine to Southern forces in her little papier-mâché head during the same war between the states, probably to supply drugs for the wounded.

(12)

(11)

(13)

Sometime in the same decade of the 1860's, a Michigan woman celebrated the victory of the Union forces by making a doll, with a papier-mâché head and a kid body, in the image of General Grant (12). On the Confederate side of the conflict, many Southern families found themselves homeless and poor for the first time. The Southern gentlewoman who made this cloth grandmother (13) supported herself by making fine cloth dolls after the war. This is the thousandth doll she made.

(14)

(15)

(16)

CLOTH DOLLS

By the end of the Civil War, the first commercially made dolls were being sold in the United States. Pattern dolls became popular and remained popular into the twentieth century. Simple doll patterns were printed on cloth and sold in yard-goods stores, where young girls bought them to sew and stuff at home. Different dolls often emerged from the same pattern. Mollie Bentley made a pattern doll in Lancaster, Pennsylvania (14), that was quite different than the doll made from the same pattern by her sister Maggie (15).

Although cloth is not as durable as wood, a cloth doll can last several generations, as it did in the family of Mrs. Martha Reed of

(17)

(18)

(19)

Kalamazoo, Michigan. Mrs. Reed made a doll called Aggie (16) in 1851, and Aggie lived in the Reed family for four generations. Her hair is made of floss. Her features are embroidered. Cloth dolls were also used as advertising promotions in the nineteenth century, as this boy doll (17) was used by the Boston Cash Register Company in the early 1800's. Boy dolls have always been rare. One of the few in the Index of American Design is Johnnie, who wears a blue challis suit, hand-tucked linens and an embroidered face. Some rag dolls wore painted features, as Susie did (18) when she was made in Santa Cruz, California, in 1860. Others had a creative twist, like the nose made out of a twist of cloth in this 1830 doll (19).

(20)

Nut and Prune Doll (B. Coker Collection)

CORN AND NUT DOLLS

While dollmakers, young and old, were making dolls of wood and cloth, other craftsmen were still using the corn and apples and nuts that were so popular among young children. The results were much more elegant than the children achieved, however, as this nut-headed Colonial gentleman (20) will testify. The cotton-picking nuthead (21) was made to represent a black field hand of the late nineteenth century.

Country children were not the only ones who played with craft dolls. A corn husk doll (22) is said to have been the favorite toy of Harry Du Pont during the Civil War. On the other hand, country people often made the most elegant of dolls. The fashionable corn husk doll with parasol and puffed sleeves (23) was owned by a Kentucky woman for fifty years, a remarkable survival rate for such a perishable material.

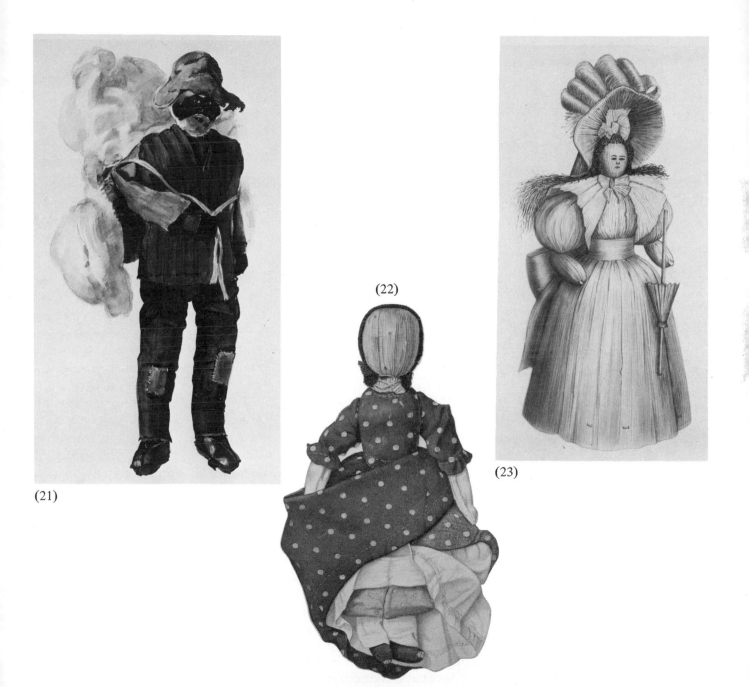

(21)

(22)

(23)

(26)

THE LOST STORY OF DOLLS

Every doll in the Index of American Design would have a story to tell if we could hear it. Who was Sadie Berman, whose face was carved in a portrait doll (24) in Massachusetts at an unknown date? Who was the Indian whose image was carved into a doll (25) by a Michigan man in the nineteenth century? Most of these questions will never be answered. The only thing we can do to identify the story of a doll is to make an educated guess based on historical information.

We know, for example, that doorstop dolls were half a rag-doll body propped on a bottle full of sand or buckshot. These dolls were used to prop open a door. We also know that photograph 26 depicts one of many doorstop dolls made by the ladies of the Episcopal Church in Hampton, Virginia. The rest of the story is gone.

Occasionally, we know the name of the dollmaker, as we do with the puppet made by John Difenderfer between 1888 and 1890. This is a Judy puppet (27), part of the famous Punch and Judy puppet shows which made dramatists and theater lovers out of children in the nineteenth century.

Not all nineteenth-century Americans had homemade dolls, of course. Dolls of many kinds were imported from Europe after 1800, and doll heads were often attached to homemade bodies. By 1858, the first American doll patent had been given to Ludwig Greiner. The United States was ready to take advantage of the Industrial Revolution, which would bring commercially made dolls to every child in the twentieth century.

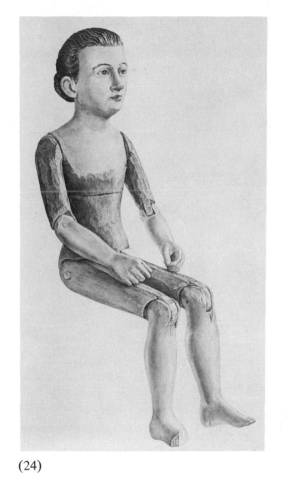

(24)

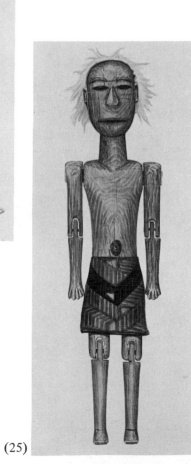

(25)

Geo. J. File

(27)

93

ROOTS OF
THE DOLL INDUSTRY

If you could focus a camera on North America in the middle of the nineteenth century, you would see a continent in which every family home contained at least one doll. In North America, as in the European "motherlands" that supplied most of our early immigrants, the affluent had sophisticated dolls expensively made of wood, wax, composition and china, with articulated bodies of cloth and kid dressed in the styles of the day. The average child had homemade dolls of rag, nut or corn, or the simple wooden dolls produced by the hands of families of European dollmakers.

European dollmaking had progressed for more than four hundred years on the concept of the individual craftsman. One man or woman worked alone to produce more and more realistic heads and bodies, first for royalty and then for the affluent. At the same time, single families, or whole villages of families, worked together in cottage industries to make wooden dolls which have been called by various names: Dutch dolls, Flanders dolls and penny woodens. These inexpensive wooden dolls were manufactured in a world of Tyrolean villages and family dollmaking businesses, where mother and father and children and relatives and friends made dolls in an "assembly line" of hands.

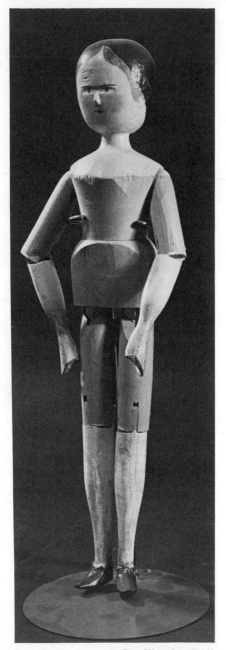

Peg Wooden Doll

It was a world of too many people and too little land, where extra hands were available to craft such objects one by one. The land, of course, usually went to the oldest son. What happened to the other children? Many of them migrated to the New World, where they struggled with the opposite problem: too few people and too much land to cultivate. European dollmakers emigrated to America, to seed the dollmaking business here, and mechanization eventually created an industry to bring fine dolls to average homes. Dollmaking was not an industry in America until just before the Civil War however; most of the dolls bought in America continued to be made in Europe, particularly in the Grödner Tal area of the Tyrolean Alps, until the twentieth century.

PEG WOODENS

An eyewitness description of the making of "peg wooden" dolls in the Grödner Tal was given in an 1875 issue of a British weekly called *Leisure Hours*. The article, entitled "A Tribe of Toymakers," was written by Margaret Howitt. It is worth looking briefly at that "tribe," because these wooden-dollmaking skills were at the root of early doll manufacture in America.

The author writes from the village of St. Ulrich (known to the local people as Ortiseit), on the Dirshingar Bach River, just twenty years after a carriage road was built to the outside world for the first time. Toymakers in this area had made wooden dolls, harlequins, wagons and farm animals for the people of Europe for two generations. The author describes a woman dabbing vermillion coloring on dolls.

"Tomorrow she will add the rosy lips, the red shoes and white stockings; the day after, the black eyes, eyebrows and hair, all forming the distinctive features which these literal "babes in the woods" must possess. She tells us Herr Purger gives her the dolls to paint. He pays her a farthing a dozen out of which she buys the paint and size. If she could work at home (she sells fruit at the hotel door too) she could paint several hundred dozen a week, but with her stall she never manages more than half the number."

It is a vivid picture of a toymaking village, in which the woman's father carves horses and dolls and her sister paints them. Long before the American Revolution, Grödner Tal doll salesmen carried great containers of toys and dolls into Italy and Spain. By the Civil War these dolls were known to English children as "Dutch dolls," probably the same distortion of the word "Deutsch," or "German," which occurred with the "Pennsylvania Dutch" in the United States. There is no evidence that these popular "Dutch" and "Flanders" dolls were actually made in the low countries of Holland and Belgium until the twentieth century.

Dollmakers in the Grödner Tal followed the same principle followed by every craftsman since the beginning of time. They used available materials and available tools within the cultural concepts of their time. "Peg wooden dolls" were literally jointed wooden dolls held together by wooden pegs. They pleased thousands of children on both sides of the Atlantic for centuries, but by the middle of the nineteenth century there were new materials and new tools available to dollmakers. Sophisticated European dolls had long been made of wax and china, and a composition of papier-mâché and other materials, but they were usually too expensive for the average family. It was the era of mechanization, and the materials and skills that grew out of it, that brought fine dolls to ordinary people.

Springfield Dolls

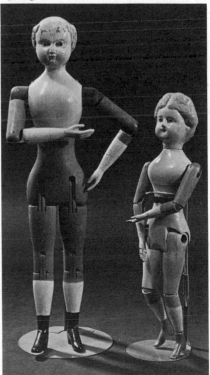

Schoenhut Dolls

Greiner Doll

THE DOLL INDUSTRY IN NORTH AMERICA

Charles Goodyear started making soft rubber toys in 1837, and his brother Nelson Goodyear patented hard rubber, which was later made into doll heads, in 1851. Molded rubber doll heads with painted faces became relatively plentiful and inexpensive, although few have survived because the rubber deteriorated and the paint peeled off.

While rubber was being developed for practical use, a German immigrant named Ludwig Greiner took out the first United States doll patent in 1858 using paper, Spanish whiting, rye flour, glue and linen cloth to mold a reinforced composition head. It is ironic that Greiner should be the first official dollmaker, because he came to the United States determined to follow any profession except the one he had learned in Europe: dollmaking. Most Greiner heads were bought and attached to homemade bodies, although there is an unverified

Leather Head

Rubber Doll

Rubber Doll Head

belief among some collectors that he may also have made commercial doll bodies.

Even wooden dolls acquired a new "industrialized" look. The American-born craftsman Joel Ellis, already a manufacturer of fine carriages and toys, patented jointed wooden dolls with pewter hands and feet. He started a dollmaking tradition in Springfield, Vermont, that was followed by such famous dollmakers as Frank Martin, George Sanders, Luke Taylor, H. H. Mason and C. C. Johnson, all of whom added new dimensions to dollmaking.

A seventeen-year-old German immigrant called Albert Schoenhut, whose family had been making dolls in Europe for a hundred years, started practicing his trade in the United States in the late nineteenth century. His swivel, spring-jointed dolls were not patented, however, until 1911.

Newspapers had also moved out of the hand press of Colonial times to the mechanized presses which mass-produced the "penny newspaper" for the great flow of European immigrants into the New World. Newspapers were the educators and taste-setters of society, so it is not surprising that a newspaper illustrator began a new rage in popular dolls. Palmer Cox, a New York City illustrator born in Granby, Quebec, began drawing good-natured fairy creatures that were to become as versatile a form of fantasy creature as Mickey Mouse became a century later. Webster defined brownie as "a good-natured goblin supposed to perform helpful services by night." Palmer Cox Brownies were reproduced in dozens of forms: pottery, stuffed dolls, and as decorations on hundreds of everyday items. The famous Brownie camera was named after the Brownie. Brownies were one of the most popular of the pattern dolls: printed cloth patterns which were sold by yard-goods stores and sewn and stuffed by small children from the last quarter of the nineteenth century until well into the twentieth century.

Brownie Pattern Dolls

Izannah Walker Doll

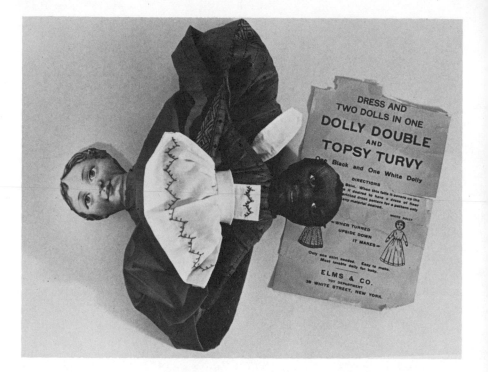

In the late nineteenth century, stuffed dolls were still the most popular little creatures to go to bed with at night, and they too were part of the early commercial doll scene. Martha Chase of Pawtucket, a Massachusetts town which has since become part of Rhode Island, wanted to make soft, cuddly dolls with flexible limbs for children. Her finely painted stockinette dolls with jointed elbows, knees and hips, and dainty toes and fingers, went commercial one day when a sales clerk noticed their potential and suggested that Mrs. Chase go into business. The business soon expanded to include both small- and full-sized demonstration dolls used to train hospital nurses.

Izannah Walker of Central Falls, Rhode Island, also adapted cloth dolls into a form now highly prized by collectors. According to her patent, she placed "several thicknesses of cotton or other cheap cloth, treated with glue or paste, so that they will adhere together and hold the shape impressed upon them by the dies." These cloth forms were dried, covered with other layers of soft materials, pressed, filled with stuffing and reinforced with a piece of wood.

Izannah Walker Doll

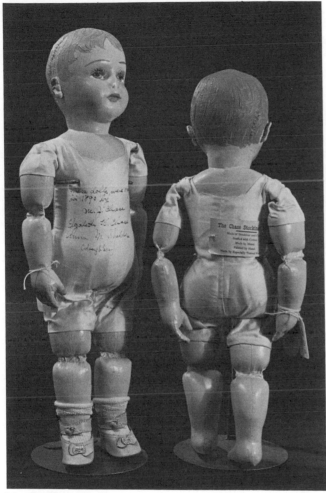
Martha Chase Dolls

Pattern Doll

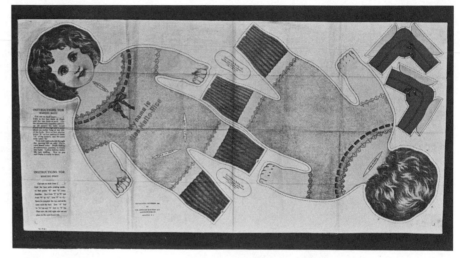

America had a doll industry at last. About one hundred and fifty patents were applied for between 1850 and 1900, although beautiful china, bisque and wax dolls continued to be imported in quantity from Europe until the flow across the Atlantic was dammed up by World War One. Many European doll factories were damaged by the war, launching America into the huge dollmaking industry it now enjoys. Dolls went on to become reflections of American life, with movie stars and famous people reproduced in their own small image, and vinyl dolls eventually becoming the companion of North American children. North American dollmaking, which had grown for three hundred years in corn fields and forests, from nut trees and rag bags, brought elegant manufactured dolls to the descendants of pioneers everywhere, but Americans and Canadians living in isolated places continued to make homemade dolls of available environmental materials.

China Head
Collection

APPALACHIA

Environmental materials are still used by the craftsmen of Appalachia, whose continuing dollmaking skills are aptly described by twentieth-century Tennessee dollmaker Helen Bullard. Mrs. Bullard is widely known as a doll expert in the United States. This is how she describes dollmaking as folk art.

"Deep in the mountains of Eastern Kentucky a woman heeds her little girl's 'keening' for a doll. The child has seen a lovely little doll in a store window in the county seat and she longs for one for her very own. What to do? There will be no trip to town again for months—not until spring. The mother hunts a white piece of wood and with her kitchen knife fashions a crude head. She digs out two holes for eyes, leaves between them a triangular mound for a nose, and below it a circular mound for a mouth. With a stub of pencil she marks out the eyebrows and adds dots for the pupils of the eyes. A doll must have hair. The mother goes to her spinning wheel and from the washed wool waiting to be spun chooses a wisp of curly black. Flour-and-water paste fasten it to the top and back of the doll's head. Arms come next, whittled with closed mitten hands from a small piece of wood. Legs need longer and larger pieces. From the ragbag come scraps of flour sack for a body to hold all these pieces together and out back is sawdust for the stuffing. Again the scrapbag is sought; it gives up scraps of printed flour sack for panties and dress. Soon a doll is born and a little mountain girl back-of-beyond has her keening stopped and her arms filled with a new little friend."

Edison Talking Doll

106

Early Walking Dolls

Appalachian Dolls

THE NOSTALGIA MAKERS

The frontier has vanished, but frontier dolls are still being made in a stainless-steel world where jet planes and concrete highways have replaced Conestoga wagons and rocky trails. Children and adults still make dolls from available materials, ranging from plastic bottles to nylon stockings, but people who like to work with their hands continue to make homemade dolls from the old materials of the land: wood, corn, nuts and rags. Crafts, which once produced the everyday goods needed by every family, have been replaced by craft hobbies, which now create dolls from the products of the earth to decorate modern homes and to go on delighting children. Children may still make these dolls, but most of the nostalgia makers are adults. Among the most prolific of the dollmakers are the corn huskers, the appleheads, the nutheads and the cloth-doll craftsmen.

CORN HUSK DOLLS

THE CORN HUSKERS

It is possible to make a corn husk doll from the corncobs you buy in the store, but it is an unsatisfactory source because the husks are often trimmed or removed. Green corn husks do not work well, and it's expensive to let the corn become inedible while husks dry around the cob at home.

The best source of corn husk is still the farmyard, where farmers let feed corn dry on the stalk. Corn should be picked after it is dried, but before fall rains can mildew the husks. Farmers will often allow you to pick and remove the husks, twisting the cobs carefully out of their casing and leaving the cobs behind for feed. There are two reasonable alternatives to farm corn: buy husks already packaged in a craft store, or buy them from Mexican food shops which stock husks for tamales.

A corn husk doll can be made by following the directions for the grass doll in Scenes of American Childhood: The husks are folded in half to make a body, the fold is stuffed and tied to make a head, and a few strands from each side are pulled out and tied back to make arms. This makes a simple, charming doll. The more complex corn husk doll shown here is made in steps: A husk is rolled and tied around wire to make arms; husks are twisted and tied to make a head; these two parts are joined and dressed in more husks to make the complete doll. A few hints make the job easier: When you tear rough edges off husks, always tear from the bottom, or coarse end, to the top; if corn husks get too dry, dampen before using; pin *across* the grain so the husk won't tear.

TO PREPARE FARM OR TAMALE CORN HUSK

Soak husks in very hot water with 1/2 cup liquid dishwashing detergent for 4 hours. Rinse. Then soak husks overnight in a gallon of very hot water mixed with 1/2 cup liquid dishwashing detergent and 1/2 cup liquid bleach. Rinse. Spread out and dry until ready to use. (Husks purchased at craft stores are already prepared to this point.)

MATERIALS FOR THE CORN HUSK DOLL

(See page 138 for discussion of materials and possible substitutions.)
Corn husks
1-1/4 cups liquid dishwashing detergent
1 ounce glycerine or 1/4 cup water softener
1/2 cup liquid bleach
5-inch length of 18-gauge florist wire
Kite string or unraveled carpet thread, dyed in hot tea
Cotton balls
Embroidery thread or corn silk
White household glue
Tools
Scissors
Straight pins
Paper cup (medium size)

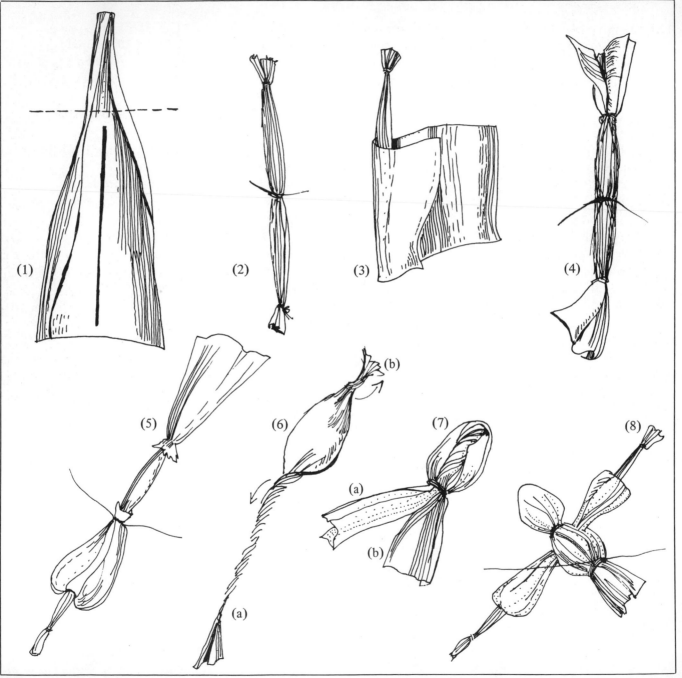

(1)

(2)

(3)

(4)

(5)

(6)
(b)
(a)

(7)
(a)
(b)

(8)

HOW TO MAKE
A CORN HUSK DOLL

• *When you are ready to use the husks,* soak them in a gallon of hot water with 1/4 cup liquid dishwashing detergent and either 1 ounce glycerine or 1/4 cup water softener until wet, about 20 minutes. The husks must be wet when making the doll.

To Make the Arms

• *Select a piece of fine corn husk 2 to 3 inches wide.* Tear off the thin strip of very coarse husk along the long edges. (Note: Always tear corn husk from the bottom, or coarse end, towards the top.)

• *Place a 5-inch wire lengthwise in husk* and trim husk 1/4 inch beyond each end of the wire (1).

• *Roll the corn husk tightly around the wire.* Tie off at both ends with string about 1/2 inch from edge, keeping knots on the same side of the roll, and then tie in center (2). (Note: It is important that all knots on the doll be tied with wet string as tightly as possible unless otherwise indicated.)

To Make the Sleeves

• *Select 2 pieces of husk* and cut them into 2 identical 3- by 4-inch pieces, with the 4-inch side running across the grain. Place 1 piece of the husk so that it extends 1/2 inch beyond center mark of arm; 1/3 is over the arm and 1/3 extends outwards (3).

• *Gather the folded 2/3 slowly* with your fingers, fold extended piece over and gather; tie. (Note: Be careful not to roll the arm as you gather or the arm will not bend properly.)

Attach other arm in the same way, gathering in the opposite direction so both edges face up as shown (4).

• *Turn 1 sleeve inside out,* puffing and smoothing with fingers, and tie just beyond center mark of arm (5).

• *Turn second sleeve and tie* over ends of first, so that only 1 tie shows. Set arm-and-sleeve piece aside while you make the head.

To Make the Head

• *Lay a piece of fine corn husk on the table.* Place 2 cotton balls on the husk 3/4 of the way towards the wide end of husk. Roll husk around cotton tightly, twisting each end of husk into tails in opposite directions like a candy kiss (6). You now have a long thin tail piece (a) and a short coarse neck piece (b). Pull the tail piece back over head, covering the seam at the back of the head. Tie the tail piece and neck piece tightly under cotton balls to form head.

• *Separate the tail piece from the neck piece (7).* Push arm-and-sleeve piece tightly up between the tail piece and the neck piece centering the arms. Stuff 2 cotton balls up inside neck piece to form bust. In order to keep doll's head upright, pull tail piece down tightly. Tie under bust to form the waist (8). Pull arms straight up so they point overhead.

(9)

(10)

To Make the Skirt

• *Select 8 to 10 coarse husks.* Cut points off husks. Choose the best husk for the skirt front. Invert head so that it is upside down, facing the skirt husk (9). You can then gather and make an inside "seam" at the waist.

Gather 1 husk at a time, tying each at the waist. As you add each new husk, overlap it halfway across the husk you have tied, so that the skirt is always a doubled thickness. Turn doll right side out, smoothing and puffing skirt at waist. Your "seam" is now inside (10).

• *Finish skirt hem in one of two ways:* (1) Gather skirt in your hand so that husks overlap, trim with scissors and tie loosely. You will remove tie when husks are dry. (2) Turn hem under 2 inches, being careful to include 2 layers of skirt all the way around, and pin horizontally across grain on the outside of skirt. Set over an inverted paper cup so that skirt will dry in an even circle. Remove pins before husk is completely dry to avoid rust marks. If skirt does not hold its shape when pins are removed, tie loosely; remove tie when skirt dries. You are now ready to add apron.

To Make the Apron

• *Choose a large piece of corn husk.* Tear it gently halfway down the center from the point of husk towards the wider end. Press the end of the V firmly with your thumb against the front of the waist so the corn will not tear farther (11).

• *Place the 2 ends over shoulder,* crossing at the back (12).

• *Tie a 1-inch-wide strip of husk* around waist as a sash. Tie sash once at the back and pin until dry. (Note: You should not try to double knot corn husks.)

Shape apron by cutting edges to a point or trimming with pinking shears. Bend and position arms.

To Make the Hair

• *Use either strands of dried corn silk which have been wetted, or a single package of embroidery thread.* Leave thread in wrapper; cut off both ends evenly. Lay corn silk threads side by side and trim ends evenly. You now have several strands bundled side by side. Comb gently with fingers to separate strands. Tie loosely in center to form part (13). Spread glue over top and upper back of head. Press hair against head with part at center. Tie a thread loosely around neck and hair to give hair shape; remove tie later. Trim hair ends.

(11)

(13)

(12)

To Make the Bonnet

- *Cut a piece off the wide end of a husk to a depth of 2 inches.* This should be long enough to go from one shoulder over the head to the other shoulder. Fold lengthwise to make poke of bonnet. Gather raw edges and tie. Turn inside out, so that knot is on inside and shape the poke around your finger (14). Place on head so that poke angles forward, and pin on each side. To make top of bonnet, measure from top of head to back of neck and add 1/4 inch. Cut a piece of husk this long and 1-1/2 inches wide. Gather both ends; tie each end. Smooth center open, knots turned under (15). Place one knotted end against bonnet at center of poke and second knotted end against back of neck. Glue poke and top of bonnet to head.

(14)

(15)

APPLEHEAD DOLLS

THE APPLEHEADS

Who first made applehead dolls? Some people believe that the Seneca Indians used them long ago as "wish dolls," but there is no more information about the origin of these dolls than there is about the origin of any of the folk dolls. Appleheads are most often made today by the craftmakers of Appalachia. Some craftsmen stuff them, some varnish them, and a few just let them rot away with time.

The applehead doll shown here is made with a carved apple that is dipped in lemon juice, dried and lightly shellacked before it is attached to a wire body that has been wrapped in strips of cloth. Note the pear dolls, which can be made the same way. We have not included directions for dressing the dolls, because doll costumes are made in basically the same way for all dolls: They are made either as a scrap dress, or cut and fitted as they would be for any adult.

MATERIALS FOR THE APPLEHEAD DOLL

(See page 138 for discussion of materials and possible substitutions.)
2 large apples
2 cloves or peppercorns for eyes
5-inch length of 18-gauge mechanics' wire or lightweight coat hanger
1 cup lemon juice
Non-iodized salt
Optional: red watercolor for face
Clear shellac
Embroidery thread for eyebrows
Embroidery thread or dacron batting for hair
White household glue
One 24-inch length and two 12-inch lengths of 18-gauge mechanics' wire or lightweight coat hanger
Several strips of stretchable cloth, i.e., an old T-shirt
Tools
Small sharp knife
Toothpicks
Styrofoam base, empty salt shaker box or extra apple
Pins
Needle and thread

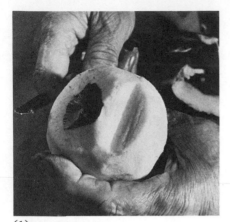

(1)

HOW TO MAKE
AN APPLEHEAD DOLL

(2)

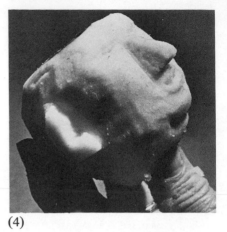

(4)

- *Peel the apple* by paring it in one continuous strip. Make the strip as thin as possible, leaving most of the pulp on the apple. Smooth the surface of the apple by gently scraping downward with a knife. Use the smoothest side for the face.
- *Form the forehead* by cutting a wedge from the top of the apple (1).
- *Carve the nose* by cutting away a small wedge on each side of the apple leaving a ridge in the center which looks like an upside-down V (2). Slice another wedge from underneath the nose, so that the nose is an appropriate length. Shape the nose by gently scraping to round and soften this feature. Care must be taken during this operation because the nose is quite fragile. Add the nostrils by gently inserting the knife tip in the bottom of the nose; scrape just enough pulp to make a very small indentation.

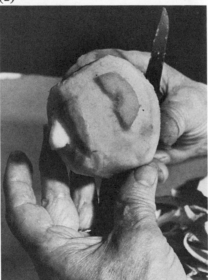

(3)

- *Carve the ears* (3). Use the ridge at the top of the nose to judge where the ears should be. Slice small pieces from the side of the head, leaving a half-moon for each ear. Scoop pulp from center of this piece, leaving a half-circle for the inner ear.
- *Draw the mouth* by making a curved line with tip of the knife, about 1/8 inch deep, under the nose. Do not remove any pulp except that which naturally clings to the knife.
- *Form the lip* by gently scraping a curved line parallel to the first underneath the mouth. As apple dries, the pulp between the 2 curved lines will form a lip. It is not necessary to draw this line exactly to the corners of the mouth (4).
- *Make eye holes* by digging gently with the tip of knife. Firmly press the selected eye materials into these holes.

120

- *Add character lines to the eyes and mouth.* For a smiling face, gently scrape away from the corners of the mouth making small lines. For twinkling eyes, make 3 lines (like bird's feet) beside each eye.
- *Finish the carving* by gently scraping with knife edge to round and smooth the head. Insert the 5-inch wire through the core of the apple. Bend the end of the wire at the chin so the apple will not slide off as it shrinks during the drying process. Bend the other end of the wire so that there is a loop from which the apple will hang while drying (5).

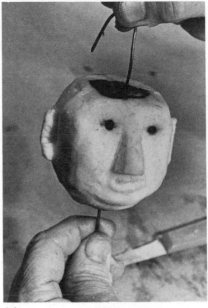

(5)

- *Dip the apple* in pure lemon juice. Sprinkle non-iodized salt liberally on it, covering it completely.
- *Dry the apple by hanging* it in a well-ventilated area (6). It should not be hung near heat, in direct sunlight or in a damp area like a basement. A north window is a good place. The average drying time is 2 to 3 weeks. In a damp climate it may take longer.
- *Decorate the head* after the applehead dries. If you wish to color the cheeks and lips, paint with red watercolor. Spray the applehead with clear shellac. Glue on embroidery thread for eyebrows. Glue on embroidery thread or dacron batting for hair.

(6)

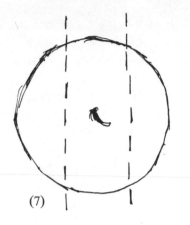

(7)

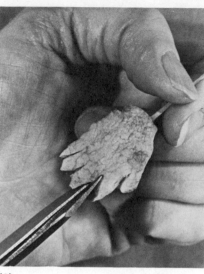

(9)

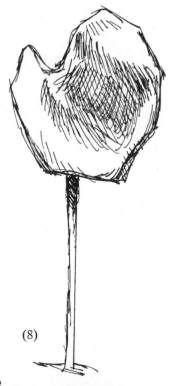

(8)

• *Form the fingers* after the mitts have dried for approximately 4 days or when the texture is spongy. Make 3 slits in each mitt with scissors (9).

To Make the Body
• *Make a wire frame for the body* by folding the 24-inch wire in half. It will look like a large hairpin (10). The open end of this folded piece will be the doll's legs and the folded end will be the neck. Cross this piece with the 12-inch piece of wire about 3 inches down from the folded end of the 24-inch piece to form the arms.

To Make the Hands
• *Peel a second apple* in the same manner as you did for head. Slice off a piece from either side (7).
• *Make mitts* by cutting a wedge in each slice to form a thumb.
• *Shape the palm* by gently scooping pulp from the middle of each mitt. Scrape edges of each piece to form the rough shape of the mitt.
• *Insert a toothpick in the bottom of each mitt.* Dip mitts in the lemon juice and sprinkle liberally with salt. Stick toothpicks into a styrofoam base (8), into holes of table salt shakers or another apple.

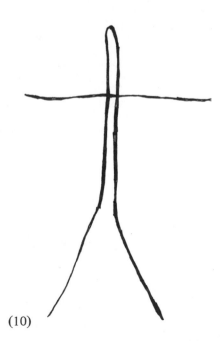

(10)

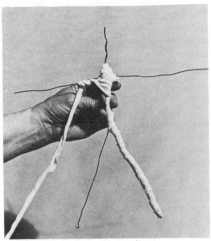

(11)

- *Bend the wire tip of each leg* to form feet and to prevent the wrapping from sliding off. Do not bend wire tip of arms.
- *Make a bustline for a woman doll (12).* Make 2 small balls, using the T-shirt strips, and pin them to the doll's chest. Wrap a strip of the material completely around the doll's chest to shape and hold bust. Sew a few stitches between the breasts to form the bust. Continue wrapping by criss-crossing the strip over the area just sewn. Secure the end of the wrapping material by tucking or sewing.

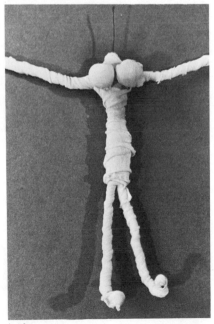

(12)

- *Begin wrapping the wires with the T-shirt strips where they cross (11):* Hold a strip of the material in place with the thumb and wrap it around each section of the crossed wires. Wrap this area several times so that the crossed wire is held firmly in place. Wrap the strip around the neck piece, about 3 times, leaving the top of the wire bare. Continue to wrap the strip down one leg, then back up to the neck again and around. Continue to wrap in this manner until both legs and both arms are covered, except 1 inch at tips of arms. As one strip of material ends, tuck a new piece under one of the folds, sew or tape it and continue to wrap.

- *Attach the head to the body.* Remove the wire from the dried applehead. Stick the neck of the body completely through applehead core. Bend the wire tip to hold the head in place.
- *Attach hands to arms.* Dress the doll before attaching the hands. Bend the wire tip of each arm. Keep hands on toothpicks on which they dried. Attach toothpicks to the wrists by wrapping with T-shirt strip or tape. Do not stick wire into hands.

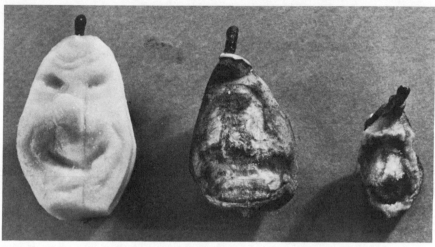

The body for an applehead doll may be made from twigs instead of wire.

Pears may be substituted for apples in making heads and carved in the same manner as appleheads. Below are simple clothes for applehead dolls from the collection of Mrs. T. Little.

NUTHEAD DOLLS

THE NUTHEADS

The nuthead is one of the most elementary and versatile folk dolls. In its simplest form shown here a hole is drilled or punched "ear to ear" so that a wire may be inserted. The wire is shaped to form the body, and the doll is dressed. Nutheads have also been attached to bodies made of dried prunes, bodies carved of wood or bodies clothed in large leaves. Nutheads have the characteristics of all folk art: Every craftsperson does it his or her own way.

MATERIALS FOR THE NUTHEAD DOLL

(See page 138 for discussion of materials and possible substitutions.)
1 walnut or other large nut
Watercolor or felt pen
One 16-inch length and one 9-inch length of 20-gauge wire or lightweight coat hanger
12-inch square of cloth
Tools
Drill, preferably 1/16 inch
Paintbrush
Pliers
Scissors

HOW TO MAKE A NUTHEAD DOLL (1)

- *To make the head,* make a hole from one side of the nut to the other with a drill or sharp tool. Paint on features.
- *To make the body,* insert the 16-inch length of wire through the holes. Center the nut on the wire. Bend wire. Twist it 6 times under the nut to form neck.
- *To make the arms,* place the 9-inch length of wire between the 2 strands of body wire and continue to twist body wire until the body is 1-1/2 inches long. Center arms. Twist arm wire twice around body to secure arms. Bend 1 inch of wire at the end of each arm to form hands. Bend arm wire at shoulders and elbows.
- *To make the legs,* bend 1/2 inch at end of each leg into a circle to make feet. Bend wire at knees.
- *Optional: Wrap body* as shown in applehead doll.

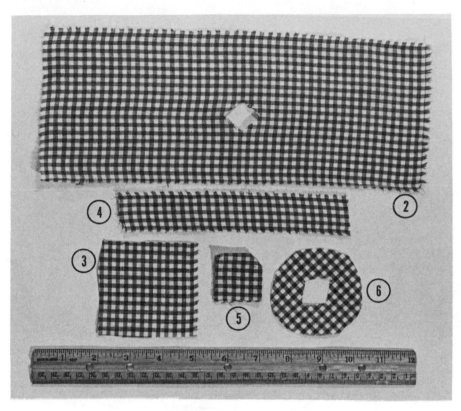

(1)

To Dress the Doll

• *Cut the 12-inch square of cloth in 3 pieces:* One 8- by 12-inch rectangle for dress (2); One 3-inch square for hat (3); One 8- by 1-inch strip for sash (4).

• *To make the hat,* fold the 3-inch square twice (5). Cut off folded corner, starting 1/4 inch down both sides from corner. You now have a square with a hole in the middle. Round corners to make hat (6). Push hat down on nuthead.

• *To make the dress,* fold the 8- by 12-inch rectangle twice, and cut hole by cutting 1/2 inch off folded corner.

• *Push nuthead through hole* in dress. Loosely arrange over wire body. Tie at waist with sash.

CLOTH DOLLS

THE CLOTH DOLLS

Cloth dolls are one of the most ancient forms of play dolls. They have been made for centuries of children. They are still made at home today. In the twentieth century, there are three common ways of making stuffed dolls:

• Most people make them from patterns, which can be purchased from a variety of pattern manufacturers. Reproductions of old doll patterns are available from specialty pattern houses. I have not tried to reproduce a doll pattern here because such patterns are available in any store that sells yard goods.

• A few mothers, who feel very comfortable with a needle and thread, still make their own cloth dolls without a pattern. The photographs and drawings in this section will give a seamstress helpful hints for making a homemade rag doll. A very simple "gingerbread man" can be made by cutting two pieces of material the rough shape of a man, sewing the pieces together and stuffing them. This doll may be too stiff, however; the floppy dolls so loved by children are made in very simple but separate parts. A single part represents the head and body. Tubular arms and legs are attached. The arms may be curved slightly or left straight.

• The simplest cloth doll is the stocking doll, which is quickly made from a pair of short socks.

129

SIMPLE RAG DOLL

The outline on this page may be used as a pattern for the head and torso of a simple rag doll. It may be enlarged by copying it onto another piece of paper with a larger grid.

Cut two pieces of cloth the shape of the outline. Sew pieces together along all edges except the bottom. Turn inside-out so the seams are inside. Stuff with rags or cotton batting and sew bottom. Make the arms and legs from straight or curved pieces of cloth. Sew them up into tubes and stuff them (1) before sewing them to the body so they will be floppy. Sew the features on the face with embroidery thread. Make hair and braids from yarn and sew onto the head. Tie with ribbon.

To make socks (2) cut the cuffs from a pair of socks and sew them into tubes. Cut off a section of the foot of the sock for underpants, slip them over the body and tack them between the legs. To make a blouse, slit a single piece of material at the center, pull it over the doll's head, gather it at the neck and seam it under the arms. To make a long skirt, sew a straight piece of material around the doll's waist. The apron and bonnet pictured here (3) were made from a pattern. A simple apron may be made by sewing a gathered piece of cloth to a ribbon and tying it around the waist.

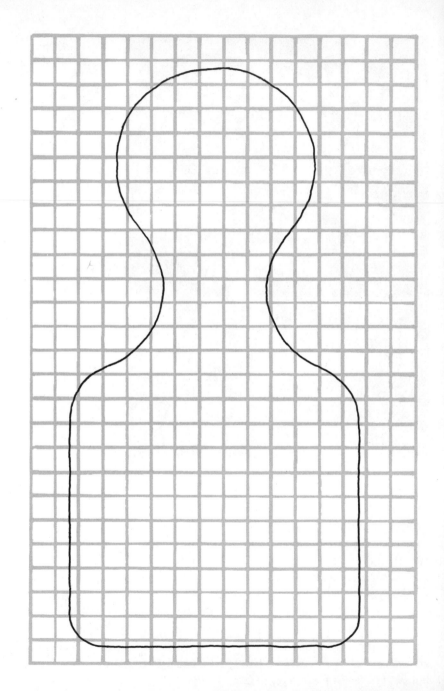

130

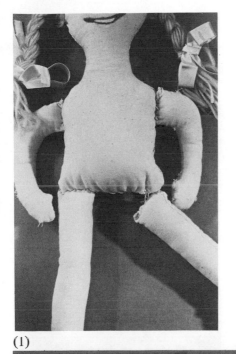

(1)

(2)

(3)

(4)

131

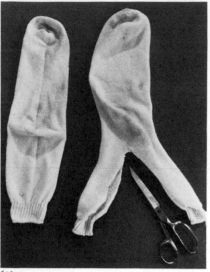

(1)

MATERIALS FOR
THE SOCK DOLL

(See page 138 for discussion of materials and possible substitutions.)

1 pair of short socks

Cotton stuffing or cotton balls

5 pieces of wool or embroidery thread

2 buttons for eyes

Embroidery thread or felt pen for mouth and other features

Optional: 3 strips of cloth for braid

Tools

Scissors

Needle and thread

HOW TO MAKE A SOCK DOLL
To Make the Legs

• *Lay a sock down on the table* so that the heel pouches upward (1). The heel will be the hips of the doll. Cut the leg of the sock up the center towards the heel. (Caution: Do not cut the leg while the sock is on its side or the legs will be in the wrong place.)

• *Stuff the foot* of the sock with cotton to form the body (2).

• *Sew the 2 cut portions* up the inside seam and along the crotch to form the legs of the doll.

• *Stuff the legs* with cotton. Sew the ends of the legs closed. Tie each leg above the cuff of the sock with wool or embroidery thread to form feet.

(3)

To Make the Head

• *Make a tight tie* with a piece of wool or embroidery thread about 4 inches down from the toe of the sock (3).

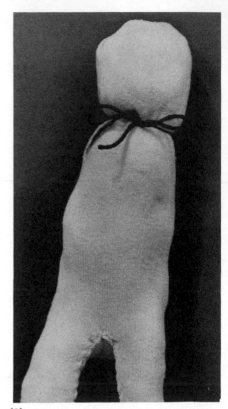

(2)

(4)

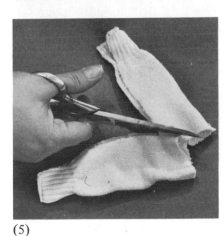

(5)

To Make the Arms
- *Cut the leg section off the second sock* by cutting across the heel portion (4). Divide this leg section in half by cutting from the cuff (5). You now have 2 pieces of sock to make arms.
- *Form each arm piece* into a tube and sew up the side. Stuff with cotton. Tie each arm above the cuff with wool or embroidery thread to form hands. Sew the arms to the side of the sock doll in the appropriate position (6).

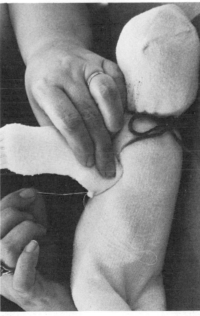

(6)

(7)

To Make the Face
- *Sew 2 buttons* on the face for eyes. Add other features with thread or felt pen.
- *You now have a boy doll.* To make a girl doll, braid 3 strips of cloth and drape across head. Sew the braids to the head (7).

Variation To make a clown, use a brightly colored sock. Add pompoms to the neck and head.

HOW TO MAKE A MONKEY DOLL

This monkey doll is a sock doll with longer, narrower arms and legs, made from a work sock with red heels. It has a long tube of sock for the tail, the heel of a second sock stuffed and added for the nose, and two small stuffed pieces for ears. The hat is a circle of sock sewn on the head.

EPILOGUE

There is a small planet called Earth that circles a star two-thirds of the way across the Milky Way galaxy. Spaceships have traveled to neighboring planets on the first step of a journey into space, but people still see their own image in the world around them. They make dolls in their own image for both ritual use and for play. Complex modern machines make vinyl dolls that would have delighted the royal doll collectors of the Middle Ages, dolls that are available to almost every child in developed societies, but there is still another secret world, a child's world, where small hands create little people that "walk" and "talk" with them in a very real living place. Like the Colonial children of New France and New England, they use simple available materials. A modern journalist, like that journalist who described an Indian child clutching a doll in sixteenth-century Virginia, could only conclude that children are still "greatlye Diligted by puppetts and babes," even when they make their babes out of a single nut, a cob of corn, an old sock or a branch from a tree.

NOTES ON MATERIALS

Homemade dolls are made of available materials. The materials available in the seventeenth and eighteenth centuries were much more limited than the materials available to us today. The directions in this book generally include reference to materials used in earlier periods of North American life, but a twentieth-century dollmaker may prefer to use more modern materials for some of the steps shown. Some of the alternatives are listed here, along with a discussion of the way in which materials are handled. Remember that children often make temporary dolls to be used for the moment and thrown away, which may prompt them to use materials with no concern for their longevity.

CORN: Corncobs can be obtained from any available corn, whether bought in the store or collected from the field. Corn husk strips that are used for tying can also be obtained from any of the variety of corn sources, as long as they are used
138

damp. The corn husks used for corn husk dolls require a more careful consideration of the source (see page 111).

MATERIAL FOR HAIR: Corn silk can be applied when it is fresh, to make straight blonde hair, although it will darken as it dries. Dried corn silk makes brown, curly hair. Embroidery thread can be bought in a variety of colors and either braided or separated into strands for hair. Rope makes either a light curly hairdo or braids. Most homes have either 1/4-inch rope, which can be divided into separate strands, or twine, which is the equivalent of one strand of 1/4-inch rope. You can also use strips of material braided for pigtails, or any other available material that appeals to your imagination, including grass.

GLUE: White household glue has been indicated in the directions because it is simple and readily available. Other glues may be used, but do not give glue to a child if it is difficult to mix,

too quick-drying or toxic. Pins or nails can sometimes be used instead of glue if the doll will not be used by a small child.

TYING MATERIALS: In most cases, you may choose between a variety of tying materials, including strips of damp corn husk, string and ribbon. Damp corn husk strips make the tightest bind when the materials must be held firmly, as in the stick or wire body. Kite string is strong and effective for most uses. Ribbon is attractive for use as sashes.

TO MARK FACIAL FEATURES: The most authentic old-fashioned material for marking features is berry stain; crush a single berry, and allow the juice to run away, so that you are dipping your brush into liquid pulp. Watercolors or a felt pen are also simple and safe for children to use. You may want to supervise a child's use of oil or acrylics. Features can also be made from scraps of cloth, or by applying cloves or peppercorns or other whole spices when the surface of the doll is appropriate.

SCRAP DRESS: A simple scrap dress is shown in the directions for the nut-head on page 127. The method shown for cutting a neck hole in the center of the cloth can also be used in directions for other dolls, although you should be careful not to make the hole too large or the doll will slip through.

TWIGS AND STICKS: Very thin twigs are usually broken from the end of a tree branch. The branch gets thicker as you get closer to the trunk. Thicker sticks and stumps can also be found on the ground.

GRASS: Green grass can be used, but it will break easily. Dried grass is stronger, but it should be dampened slightly before use. Raffia is not a North American grass, but many doll-makers use it because it is flexible and strong (see pages 52 and 54). Raffia can be bought in any craft store.

DOLL CLOTHES: The dolls that children make are often made the simplest way. Children turn under the raw edges of material rather than hemming it. If you wish to make properly sewn doll clothes, use any available pattern, or sew tucks and seams to fit the material to the body. The rag doll shown on page 131 was dressed that way.

COTTON BALLS, which are used to stuff doll heads or to shape the body, can be purchased as balls or made by taking a handful of cotton batting, or the sterile cotton sold in drug stores, and rolling the cotton into balls about 1-1/2 inches in diameter.

WIRE: The most important criterion in selecting wire to use for making dolls is that it be easy to form into the desired shape. Florist wire, mechanics' wire and lightweight coat hanger lengths can often be used interchangeably for making the dolls in this book.

INDEX

BIOGRAPHICAL NOTES

ABOUT THE AUTHOR
Iris Sanderson Jones began her writing career as a reporter for the *Vancouver Daily Province* in Vancouver, British Columbia. She now works as a writer and consultant in a variety of creative fields. Her articles appear regularly in both newspapers and magazines. She was the first woman ever asked to teach in the Journalism Department at Wayne State University in Detroit. She is "literature advisor" to the Michigan Council for the Arts. Her work also includes lectures, travel columns, conference planning, scripts, educational comics. Mrs. Jones is a member of the American Society of Journalists and Authors, the Detroit Women Writers, Women in Communication and the Midwest Travel Writers. This book reflects her active interest in people, whose lives are inevitably designed by their physical and cultural environment.

ABOUT THE ARTIST
Catherine Claytor-Becker received both a master of arts and master of fine arts degree in printmaking from Wayne State University in Detroit, where she has taught drawing since 1972. Her work has been exhibited in numerous juried and invitational exhibitions throughout the Midwest and has received several awards.

ABOUT THE PHOTOGRAPHER
Micky Jones has been taking pictures since high school days and was a staff news photographer on the *Vancouver (B.C.) Sun* for four years while earning a degree in mechanical engineering. A Ford Motor Company manufacturing engineer for the past 25 years, Micky has maintained his interest in photography as a hobby and specializes in travel slides. He frequently collaborates with Iris to produce illustrated newspaper and magazine articles.